KT-448-625

Contents at a Glance

Table of Contents

3 Working with Group Cards   53

4 Embedding Content in a Sway   71

5 Working with Sway Charts   87

About the Author

Patrice-Anne Rutledge is a business technology author and journalist who writes about business applications, social media, and small business technology. In addition to her current book on Sway, she is also the author of numerous other books on Microsoft applications, including *Easy Office 2016*, *Easy Office 2013*, *Office 2013 All-In-One Absolute Beginner's Guide*, *PowerPoint 2013 Absolute Beginner's Guide*, and *Using PowerPoint 2010*, all from Pearson. She can be reached through her website at www.patricerutledge.com.

Dedication

To my family, with thanks for their ongoing support and encouragement.

Acknowledgments

Special thanks to Michelle Newcomb, Joyce Nielsen, Anne Goebel, Tonya Simpson, Todd Brakke, and Christopher Parent for their feedback, suggestions, and attention to detail.

We Want to Hear from You!

As the reader of this book, *you* are our most important critic and commentator. We value your opinion and want to know what we're doing right, what we could do better, what areas you'd like to see us publish in, and any other words of wisdom you're willing to pass our way.

We welcome your comments. You can email or write to let us know what you did or didn't like about this book—as well as what we can do to make our books better.

Please note that we cannot help you with technical problems related to the topic of this book.

When you write, please be sure to include this book's title and author as well as your name and email address. We will carefully review your comments and share them with the author and editors who worked on the book.

Email: feedback@quepublishing.com

Mail: Que Publishing
ATTN: Reader Feedback
800 East 96th Street
Indianapolis, IN 46240 USA

Reader Services

Register your copy of *My Office Sway* at quepublishing.com for convenient access to downloads, updates, and corrections as they become available. To start the registration process, go to quepublishing.com/register and log in or create an account*. Enter the product ISBN 9780789755438 and click Submit. When the process is complete, you will find any available bonus content under Registered Products.

*Be sure to check the box that you would like to hear from us to receive exclusive discounts on future editions of this product.

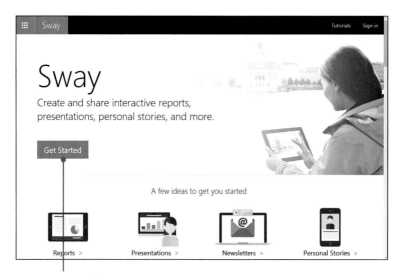

Getting started
with Sway

Prologue

In this prologue, you learn about Sway—the cloud-based app that helps you create and share multimedia content on the Web and mobile devices. Topics covered include the following:

- Understanding what you can create with Sway

- Exploring the types of content you can include in a Sway

- Enhancing your Sway with customizable styles

What Is Sway?

Sway (https://sway.com), introduced as a free preview from Microsoft in October 2014, is a web-based app that enables you to create multimedia presentations, called Sways, using any browser on your personal computer (PC), Mac, or tablet. Sway also offers apps for Windows 10, the iPhone, and iPad.

Microsoft refers to Sway as an interactive, web-based canvas. Using a variety of visual tools, you can place images, audio, video, and other content on a Sway storyline. When you're finished creating, you can make your Sway public or provide a link only to selected people.

Sway does share some similarities with Microsoft PowerPoint, but it's not just a simplified version of that presentation tool. With PowerPoint, the main focus is to create slides that supplement an in-person or web-based presentation (although its usage has expanded beyond this in recent years). A Sway, on the other hand, offers more flexible formats and is designed to be viewed on the Web without a presenter or narration.

What You Can Create with Sway

Because Sway is a flexible app, you're in control of the content, layout, and overall appearance of each Sway you create. For example, you can create a slideshow-style Sway or create a Sway that's a single page (similar to a one-page website). In addition to creating a Sway from scratch, you can also import an existing file. Supported file types include .docx (Word), .pptx (PowerPoint), or .pdf (Portable Document Format).

Although you can create a Sway on your own, Microsoft offers many collaborative features that make it easy to create and edit Sways with other people. For example, you could create a live, group Sway as a classroom activity, as a supplement to a conference or event, or as part of a corporate brainstorming session.

You can create Sways for business, school, or nonprofits—or just for your family and friends. Here's a brief list of ideas for using Sway:

- **Business reports, presentations, and newsletters**—Design a Sway highlighting a new product or service and share with customers on your website, Facebook, and Twitter. Or, use Sway to create an internal report compiled from a variety of multimedia sources.

- **Classroom projects, presentations, and activities**—Working alone or in student groups, create a Sway related to a current area of study to reinforce learning. Alternatively, use Sway to publish interactive reports for parents on student activities or share content related to a school club or project.

- **Multimedia content for family and friends**—Share a special event, reunion, party, or vacation with a Sway filled with photos, videos, and personal messages.

- **Community and nonprofit reports, presentations, and newsletters**—Share your organization and its projects with the community, potential sponsors, and the public.

Need Some Sway Inspiration?

Because Sway is a new app, you might need a little inspiration to discover its full potential. Check out the sample Sways from businesses, schools, and non-profits on the Sway website (https://sway.com). The Sway blog (blogs.office.com/product/sway), Twitter page (www.twitter.com/sway), and Facebook page (www.facebook.com/OfficeSway) also include links to interesting, creative Sways.

Content You Can Include in a Sway

Sway enables you to incorporate a variety of content into your storyline, such as images, audio, video, social media posts, maps, and more. In addition to uploading content from your computer, you can insert content from the following sources:

- OneDrive
- OneNote
- Facebook
- Flickr
- Bing
- PicHit.Me
- YouTube
- Twitter

What's PicHit.Me?

PicHit.Me (www.pichit.me) is a site you might not be familiar with. It's a global photo market and Microsoft partner that makes millions of photos available to Microsoft users. You can search the PicHit.Me library from within Sway to find potential pictures to add to your storyline.

On the storyline, you can design your Sway using content cards. These cards include layouts for text, headings, pictures, videos, tweets, and embedded content.

What Can I Embed?

You can embed videos, audio files, images, maps, charts, and documents in Sway. Supported sources include Channel 9, Docs.com, Flickr, GeoGebra, Giphy, Google Maps, Infogr.am, Mixcloud, Office Mix, OneDrive (Word, PowerPoint, Excel, PDF), Sketchfab, SoundCloud, Sway, Vimeo, Vine, and YouTube.

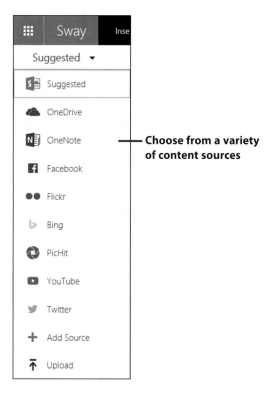

Choose from a variety
of content sources

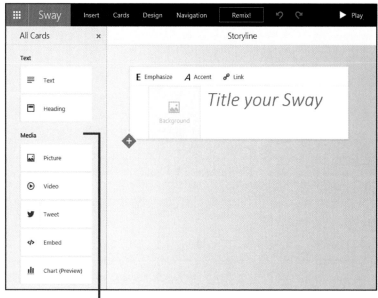

Quickly add
content with cards

Enhance Your Sway with Customizable Styles

Sway offers a collection of ready-made styles that include coordinated colors, typography, and textures. Optionally, you can customize any style with your own choice of fonts and color palette.

If you're feeling adventurous, you can let Sway do the styling for you by choosing the Remix! option, which applies a random style. If the remix isn't to your liking, click the Remix! button again to try out another style.

My Office Sway is designed to get you up and running with Sway as quickly as possible. After reading this prologue, you should have a good idea of what Sway can do and are probably eager to create your own Sways. For now, turn to Chapter 1, "Getting Started with Office Sway," to begin your adventure with this powerful communication tool.

Sway Enhancements

Be aware that as a web-based app, the Sway features available to you might vary at any given time as Microsoft continues to roll out enhancements.

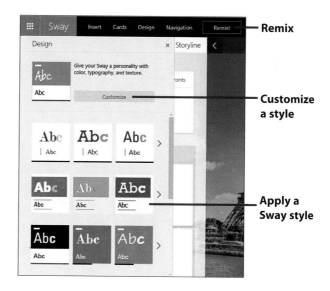

Sway menu

More options

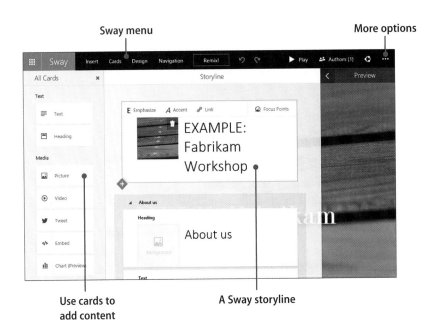

Use cards to
add content

A Sway storyline

In this chapter, you discover how to create a free Sway account, create and import Sways, and explore Sway navigation. Specific topics in this chapter include the following:

→ Creating a Sway account

→ Finding your way around Sway

→ Creating a new Sway

→ Signing in and out of Sway

Getting Started with Office Sway

Getting started with Sway is easy—sign up using your Microsoft account and begin designing. You can create a Sway from scratch or convert a Word document, PowerPoint presentation, or PDF to Sway. If you're not sure where to begin, view sample Sways to discover how they were designed and use these for inspiration or as a template for your own Sways.

Creating a Sway Account

Creating an account on Sway is a simple, straightforward process. All you need is a Microsoft account and access to the Internet through your computer or iOS mobile device.

Create a Sway Account

You can quickly create a free account on Sway (https://sway.com). When you create your account, you open a blank Sway canvas at the same time.

Sway Versus Sway
Remember that both the application and the content you create with it are called Sway. You use Sway to create a Sway.

1. Navigate to https://sway.com in your browser, and then click the Get Started button.

Learn More About Sway
The Sway home page includes a short introduction to Sway as well as some sample Sways to provide some design inspiration (scroll through the Real Sways by Real People section to view them).

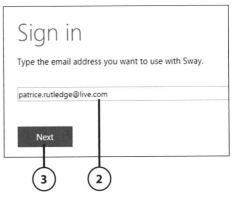

2. Enter the email address of the Microsoft account you want to use with Sway.

3. Click the Next button.

4. Enter your password.

5. If you want to remain signed in, select the Keep Me Signed In check box.

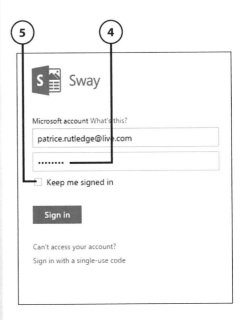

Should You Stay Signed In?

Only select the Keep Me Signed In check box if you're using your own computer that no one else has access to. Don't select this option if you're using a public computer.

6. Click the Sign In button.

7. Click the Get Started button.

8. The My Sways page opens, with sample Sways displayed.

Microsoft Account

Sway requires a free Microsoft account to access. If you have an existing account with another Microsoft application, such as Windows 10, Windows 8, Office 365, Skype, Outlook.com, Xbox Live, or Hotmail, you already have an account. In addition, you can use an email address you have linked to your Microsoft account, such as a Gmail address. If you don't have an account, you can sign up for one at http://www.microsoft.com/account.

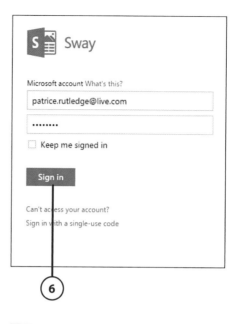

Finding Your Way Around Sway

Before creating your first Sway, take a few minutes to view some sample Sways, explore the Sway menu structure, and discover how to get help and give feedback.

Explore Sample Sways

To get a better idea of Sway in action, check out the sample Sways in your account.

1. Click Sway, if you aren't already on the My Sways page.

2. Click the sample Sway you want to open. Samples are prefaced with the word EXAMPLE.

Learn More About Sway

In addition to the sample Sways, Microsoft includes two instructional Sways (How to Start a Sway and Welcome to Sway!), which provide more information for new users.

---

3. The storyline for the sample Sway opens.

4. Scroll down the right side of the page to see each section and the cards it contains.

5. Click Preview.

6. The Preview window shows the Sway as others would see it.

7. If available, use the navigation buttons to scroll through the Sway.

Navigate a Sway

If a Sway uses the horizontal or optimized for presentation layout, navigation buttons appear in the lower-right corner that enable you to move from screen to screen. Sways with a vertical layout don't have these buttons; you scroll down them as you would any other long web page.

Use a Sample as a Template

If you want to use one of the sample Sways as a template for your own Sway, you can duplicate it. See "Duplicate a Sway" in Chapter 7, "Modifying a Sway," for more information. Just remember to replace all the existing content with your own!

Navigate Sway

Navigating Sway is a straightforward process after you understand its menu structure. The Sway menu options include the following:

- **Sway**—Open the My Sways page where you can access the Sways you've created as well as any sample Sways Microsoft provides.

- **Insert**—Insert content from OneDrive, OneNote, Facebook, Flickr, Bing, PicHit, YouTube, or Twitter. Optionally, upload content from your computer.

- **Cards**—Insert a content card such as Text, or a Heading, Picture, Video, Tweet, or Embed card.

- **Design**—Add design elements with color, typography, and texture.

- **Navigation**—Specify how you want others to navigate your Sway by selecting a layout. Currently, only three options are available: a vertical layout similar to a one-page website, a panorama layout similar to a slideshow, and a layout that's optimized for presentation.

- **Remix!**—Apply a new design automatically. If you don't like the new look, you can click Remix! again for another option or click Undo to return to your previous look.

- **Undo**—Undo the last action.

- **Redo**—Repeat the last action.

- **Play**—Preview what your Sway will look like when published.

- **Authors**—View current authors or share an edit link with others.

- **Share**—Share your Sway with the public, through social media channels (Facebook, Twitter, and more), or via a link you can provide to specific people. Optionally, you can also embed your Sway on a website.

- **More Options**—Watch tutorial videos, view the My Sways page, create a new Sway, duplicate the current Sway, provide feedback, or sign out.

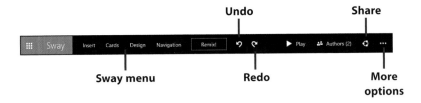

Office App Switcher

To the left of the Sway menu is the Office App Switcher, a large square with nine small squares inside it. You can click this to leave Sway and go to another Office application, such as Word, PowerPoint, or Excel.

Get Help

If you need help with doing something in Sway, particularly using a new feature not covered in this book, you can access online help.

1. Click More Options (…).

2. Select Feedback.

3. Click the Help and How-to Articles link.

Sway Community Forum

Another option for help is the Sway community forum. In this forum, you can view answers to questions related to Sway or ask your own question. Access the forum by clicking the Find Answers in the Sway Community Forum link on the Feedback page.

4. Online help for Sway displays.

5. Click the Close Tab icon (x) to close the Help tab.

6. Click the Sway tab to return to Sway.

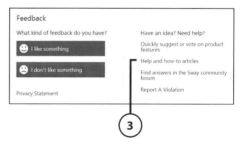

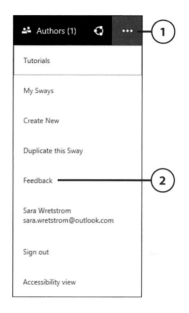

Provide Feedback

If you like something about Sway—or don't like something—you can easily let Microsoft know your opinion. Suggesting new features is another feedback option.

1. Click More Options (…).

2. Select Feedback.

3. Click either the I Like Something button or the I Don't Like Something button depending on your feedback.

4. Enter your feedback in the text box.

5. Click the Submit button.

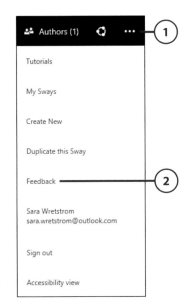

Suggest Product Features

You can have your say in the development of new Sway features by clicking the Quickly Suggest or Vote on Product Features link on the Feedback page.

Don't Want to Give Feedback?

If you decide you don't want to give feedback, press the Esc key to close the Feedback window without submitting anything.

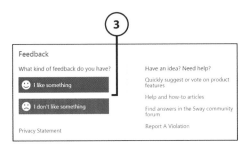

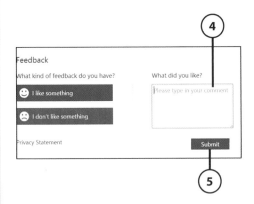

Creating a New Sway

You can create a new Sway from scratch or by importing existing content from another application.

Duplicate a Sway

Another way to create a new Sway is to duplicate a Sway you already created and then modify it. See "Duplicate a Sway" in Chapter 7 for more information.

Create a New Sway from Scratch

The most common way to create a new Sway is from scratch. You start with a blank canvas and add your own text and media files.

1. Click Sway if you aren't already on the My Sways page.

2. Click Create New. Note that there are two options for this on the screen.

3. A blank Sway storyline with a title card opens; enter a title for your new Sway.

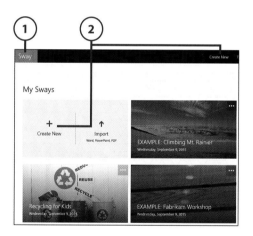

Sway Titles

Even if you don't add a title, your Sway is saved with the title Untitled and the date you created it. Don't worry too much about a title at this stage. You might even want to create a test Sway to begin with so that you can learn more before creating a Sway you want to share with others.

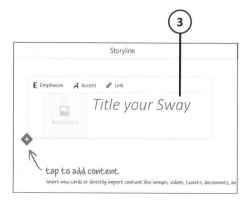

Where Is the Save Button?

If you're used to working with another Office application, you might wonder where the Save button is. Sway continuously saves your content without any action on your part, so there is no need for a Save button.

Create a New Sway by Importing Content

You can import existing content from Word, PowerPoint, or a PDF. Sway converts this content into cards on the storyline, which you can then modify.

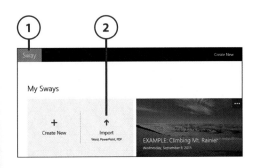

1. Click Sway, if you aren't already on the My Sways page.

2. Click Import.

3. In the Open dialog box, select the file you want to import.

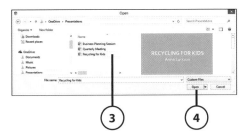

4. Click the Open button.

5. Sway displays the imported content on a new storyline; edit this content as desired.

Preview Your Imported Sway

Be sure to preview your imported Sway by clicking Preview. By previewing, you can see whether the content imported as expected and determine what modifications you need to make.

It's Not All Good

Importing Limitations

Not all content converts well to the Sway format. For example, each PowerPoint slide normally converts to a storyline card in Sway. A Word document with extensive text, however, might not convert as well. You can always try importing and then analyze the results. If they won't work without major modification, you might be better off creating your Sway from scratch. To delete an imported Sway that didn't convert properly, see "Delete a Sway" in Chapter 7.

Signing In and Out

One of the benefits of using Sway is the ability to access it from any computer, tablet, or smartphone. As long as you have an Internet connection, you can sign in to Sway. You can also sign out when you no longer want to work with your account.

Sign In to Sway

After creating a Sway account, you can sign in at any time at https://sway.com.

1. Click Sign In.

2. Enter your email address.

3. Click the Next button.

4. Enter your password.

5. If you want to remain signed in, select the Keep Me Signed In check box.

6. Click the Sign In button.

7. View the My Sways page, where you can create a new Sway or open an existing one.

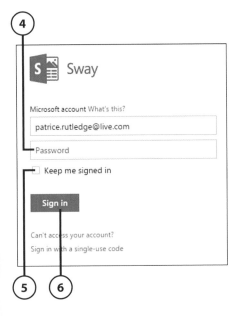

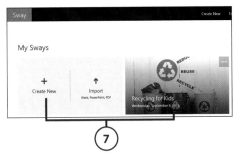

Sign Out of Sway

If you're using Sway on a public computer or a computer that other people have access to, you should sign out of your account when you're finished. Otherwise, you might want to stay signed in.

1. Click More Options (…).

2. Select Sign Out.

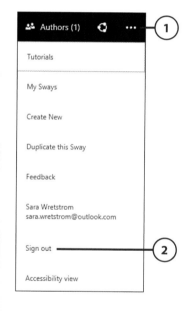

Cards menu tab

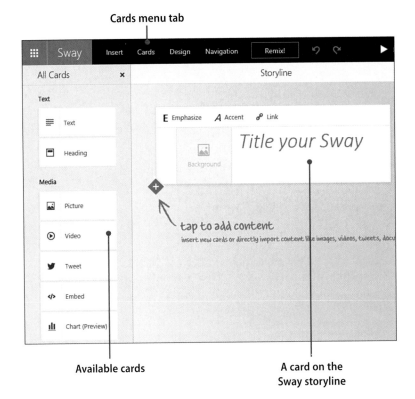

Available cards

A card on the
Sway storyline

In this chapter, you discover how to plan your Sway and explore Sway basics including layouts and cards. Specific topics in this chapter include the following:

→ Planning your Sway storyline

→ Working with navigational layouts

→ Adding content with cards

→ Working with Title Cards and Heading Cards

→ Adding text, pictures, videos, and tweets

→ Formatting text and pictures

Planning and Creating a Sway

Working with Sway starts with a plan: determining the text, pictures, videos, and other content you want to include. From there, you create a Sway and start adding this content using a series of cards.

Cards are the building blocks of Sway. Different cards hold different types of content, such as a Title Card, Video Card, or Text Card. Using a drag-and-drop interface, you add cards to a storyline and then insert content into these cards. To start, explore the basic cards such as those that enable you to add text, pictures, and videos. From there, you can add more complex cards that are covered in later chapters.

Planning Your Sway Storyline

Before you start adding cards to your Sway, it's a good idea to create a plan. Having a solid plan makes creating a quality Sway much easier. Here's a seven-step process to get you started making great Sways.

1. **Choose a navigation structure**—Sway offers three choices currently—Scrolls Vertically, Scrolls Horizontally, or Optimized for Presentation—with more options in development. See "Working with Navigational Layouts" later in this chapter.

2. **Create sections**—Sway Heading Cards function as section headers. Dividing your Sway into sections makes it easier to manage and edit. See "Add a Heading Card" later in this chapter.

3. **Add cards to your storyline**—Familiarize yourself with the available cards and determine which ones you want to use in your Sway. This chapter shows you how to add basic cards to your storyline. Later chapters show you how to add group cards (Chapter 3, "Working with Group Cards"), the Embed Card (Chapter 4, "Embedding Content in a Sway"), and the Chart Card (Chapter 5, "Working with Sway Charts").

4. **Add content to your cards**—The Add Content pane makes it easy to add content from a variety of sources. This pane opens automatically when you click various options on a card (such as clicking the Add a Picture button). This chapter introduces you to the Add Content pane, but Chapter 6, "Inserting Media Content," covers its many features in more detail.

5. **Apply a design**—Sway offers a collection of ready-made designs with matching color schemes, typography, and textures. Optionally, you can customize a design or let Sway apply a random design. See Chapter 7, "Modifying a Sway," for more details.

6. **Preview your Sway and make any adjustments**—You can quickly preview your Sway on the canvas by clicking the Toggle icon. You can also preview your Sway exactly as others see it as described in Chapter 7.

7. **Share with the world, or just selected people**—Sways are meant to be shared. To discover sharing options, see Chapter 8, "Sharing a Sway."

Sections make
it easier to
manage your
Sway

Create a Test Sway

Before creating a Sway you plan to share with others, it's a good idea to create a
test Sway while you're learning how to use this new app. Try out cards, practice
adding and embedding content, and apply new designs. After developing your
Sway skills, you'll be better prepared to create a Sway you want to share.

>>>Go Further
WHAT CAN I ADD TO A SWAY?

Knowing the available content options can help you plan a better Sway, particularly if you're new to the app. Here's a quick list of all Sway cards, sources
you can insert from, and sites you can embed from. You explore these options
in more detail later in this book, but for now, use this list as a planning
resource for your first few Sways.

You can add the following cards:

- Title
- Text
- Heading
- Picture
- Video
- Tweet
- Embed

- Chart
- Automatic (group)
- Stack
- Comparison
- Slideshow
- Grid

Be aware that the Title Card is the default card that displays at the top of the storyline of every new Sway you create. It's a required element; you can't delete it and you can't add another.

You can add content from the following sources:

- OneDrive
- OneNote
- Facebook
- Flickr
- Bing Image Search
- PicHit.Me
- YouTube
- Twitter

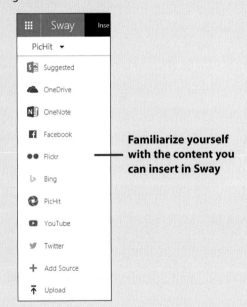

Familiarize yourself with the content you can insert in Sway

You can embed content from the following sites:

- Channel 9
- Docs.com
- Flickr
- GeoGebra
- Giphy
- Google Maps
- Infogr.am
- Mixcloud
- Office Mix

- OneDrive (Word, Excel, PowerPoint, and PDF documents)
- Sketchfab
- SoundCloud
- Sway
- Vimeo
- Vine
- YouTube

You can also upload files from your computer.

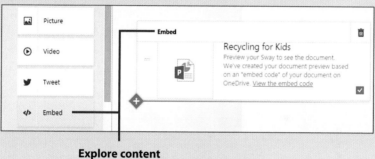

**Explore content
you can embed**

Working with Navigational Layouts

Sway offers a choice of three navigational layouts:

- **Scrolls Vertically**—Viewers scroll down your Sway as a single page, similar to a one-page website. This is the default layout.

- **Scrolls Horizontally**—Viewers scroll screen by screen, similar to a slideshow, with one or more cards displaying per screen. This layout includes buttons in the lower-right corner of the screen to navigate through the Sway.

- **Optimized for Presentation**—Viewers see each card on a separate screen. This option also includes navigation buttons in the lower-right corner of the screen.

Scrolling vertically

The same Sway scrolling horizontally

Navigation buttons

**The same Sway optimized for
presentation, one card per screen**

Navigation buttons

Apply a New Layout

If you don't want to use the default layout, apply a new one before you start adding cards to your storyline. You can always change this later, but it's best to design and preview your Sway with your preferred layout.

1. Click the Navigation tab.

2. Select the layout you want to apply.

3. Click Close (x).

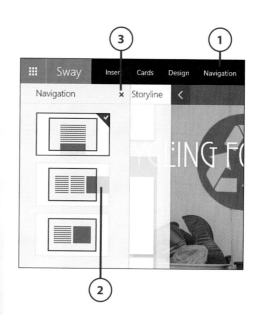

Adding Content with Cards

You add content to your Sway storyline using cards. Sway cards enable you to add headings, text, pictures, videos, audio files, tweets, and more. The advantage to using cards is that you can easily move, group, and delete them on the storyline.

You can add cards in two ways: using the Insert Content icon (text, headings, pictures, and file uploads only) or using the All Cards pane (all available cards). This section briefly shows you how each option works. Later sections show you how to add each card type in more detail.

Insert Content Using the Insert Content Icon

The Insert Content icon looks like a plus sign and enables you to quickly add content to the storyline.

1. Click the Insert Content icon.

2. Click Heading to insert a Heading Card.

3. Click Text to insert a Text Card.

4. Click Picture to insert a Picture Card.

5. Click Upload to upload a file to the storyline.

6. Click ... to open the All Cards pane.

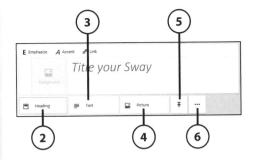

Add Content Using the All Cards Pane

You can add content from all available cards using the All Cards pane.

1. Click the Cards tab if the All Cards pane isn't already open.

2. Drag the desired card to the storyline.

Drag, Tap, or Click?

You can add a card to the storyline by dragging, tapping, or clicking it in the All Cards pane. Dragging enables you to position a card exactly where you want it. Clicking positions it after the currently selected card. If you're using a mobile device, tapping performs the same function as clicking on a desktop computer.

3. The card displays on the storyline.

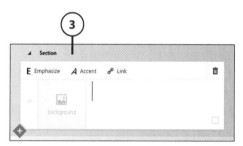

Working with Title Cards and Heading Cards

When you create a new Sway, the storyline opens and a blank Title Card displays. You can't add your own Title Card or delete the default Title Card. It's the only card that's required on every Sway.

Heading Cards form the structure of your Sway and create sections on the storyline. Sections make it easier to organize a Sway, particularly one with many cards and lots of content. You can also move entire sections rather than moving individual cards if you need to make modifications.

Modify the Title Card

In addition to adding a title to the Title Card, you can also emphasize or accent the text, add a link, or add a background picture. Emphasizing text and adding a background are most common with a Title Card.

1. Click Title Your Sway.

2. Type your title.

3. Click the Emphasize (E) button to make selected text stand out.

4. Click the Accent (A) button to make selected text more subtle.

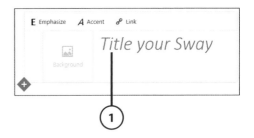

What Are the Emphasize and Accent Buttons?

The Emphasize and Accent buttons control the appearance of selected text and work differently from similar buttons in other Office applications. See the "Emphasize or Accent Text" section later in this chapter for more information.

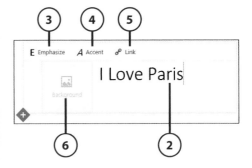

5. Click the Link button to add a hyperlink to selected text.

6. Click Background to apply a background to your Title Card. See "Apply a Background" later in this chapter for more information.

How Do I Save My Work?

Remember that Sway doesn't have a Save button. Sway continuously saves your content without any action on your part so there is no need for a Save button.

Add a Heading Card

Next, you should add your headings based on the plan you created in the previous section. Headings enable you to break up your Sways into sections.

In addition to adding a heading to the Heading Card, you can also format it, add a link, or add a background image.

1. Click the Cards tab.

2. Drag the Heading Card to the storyline.

Another Way to Add a Heading Card

Remember that you can also add a Heading Card using the Insert Content icon (plus sign) on the storyline. See "Insert Content Using the Insert Content Icon" earlier in this chapter for more information.

3. Click the Heading Card.

4. Type your heading text.

5. Click the Emphasize (E) button to make selected text stand out. See "Emphasize or Accent Text" later in this chapter to discover how these options work in Sway.

6. Click the Accent (A) button to make selected text more subtle.

7. Click the Link button to add a hyperlink to selected text.

8. Click Background to apply a background to your section heading. See the next section, "Apply a Background," for more information.

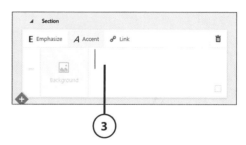

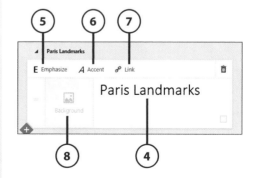

Oops!

If you don't like the Heading Card you added, you can delete it (or any other card except the Title Card). Simply select the card on your storyline and click the Delete icon (small trash can) in the upper-right corner.

Apply a Background

You can apply a background image to either a Title Card or a Heading Card. Options include a picture stored on your computer or OneDrive or a picture from Flickr, PicHit.Me, or Bing Image Search. See Chapter 6 to learn more about picture source options in Sway.

In this example, you use a picture stored on OneDrive as your background.

1. In a Title Card or Heading Card, click Background.

2. In the Add Content pane, click the down arrow to select a source. In this case, select OneDrive.

3. Drag the background picture to the card.

4. Click Close (x) to close the pane.

Delete a Background

If you don't like the background you added, you can delete it. Click the background picture on the card and click the Delete icon (a small trash can).

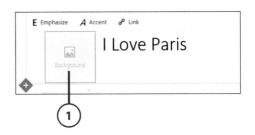

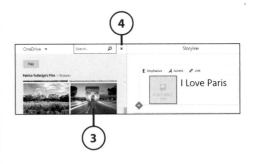

5. Click Preview.

6. Sway hides the storyline and displays the background picture on the canvas.

Return to the Storyline

To return to the storyline, click the Open Storyline button. When you return to the storyline, this button becomes the Close Storyline button. You can use this as a toggle to go back and forth between the storyline and the canvas as you design your Sway. Clicking Preview also closes the storyline.

Open Storyline

Adding Other Content Cards

In this section, you explore four other popular Sway cards: the Text Card, Picture Card, Video Card, and Tweet Card.

Add a Text Card

Adding text is a key component to any Sway.

1. Click the Cards tab.

2. Drag the Text Card to the storyline.

Another Way to Add a Text Card

Remember that you can also add a Text Card using the Insert Content icon (plus sign) on the storyline. See "Insert Content Using the Insert Content Icon" earlier in this chapter for more information.

3. Sway inserts the card in the location you specified.

4. Type your text.

Copy and Paste

You can also copy and paste text from another application, such as Microsoft Word. Because Sway doesn't currently have a spell checker, it can be useful to check your spelling and grammar in Word before adding any text sections to Sway.

5. Click the Heading button to make the text a heading. Sway moves the text to a Heading Card preceding the Text Card.

6. Click the Emphasize (E) button to make selected text stand out.

7. Click the Accent (A) button to make selected text more subtle.

8. Click the Bullet List button to apply a bulleted list to selected text.

9. Click the Numbered List button to apply a numbered list to selected text.

10. Click the Link button to add a hyperlink to selected text.

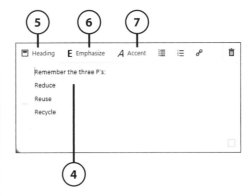

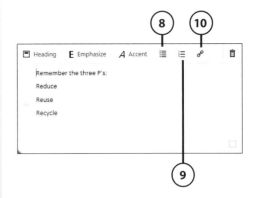

Format Text

You can apply formatting such as text emphasis, accents, bullets, or links to multiple cards that contain text, not just the Text Card. See "Formatting Text and Pictures" later in this chapter for more details.

Add a Picture Card

You can use the Picture Card to add pictures from a variety of sources including your computer, your OneDrive account, Flickr, PicHit.Me, or Bing Images. See Chapter 6 for more information about picture sources in Sway. In this example, you add a Picture Card with a picture from the PicHit.Me photo market.

1. Click the Cards tab.

2. Drag the Picture Card to the storyline.

Another Way to Add a Picture Card

Remember that you can also add a Picture Card using the Insert Content icon (plus sign) on the storyline. See "Insert Content Using the Insert Content Icon" earlier in this chapter for more information.

3. Click Add a Picture.

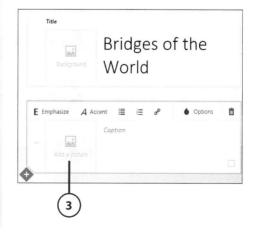

4. In the Add Content pane, click the down arrow to select a source. In this case, select PicHit.

5. Enter a keyword and click the Search button. In this example, you search for **Golden Gate Bridge**.

6. Drag the picture to the card.

7. Click Close (x) to close the pane.

8. Enter an optional caption. See "Formatting Text and Pictures" for caption formatting options.

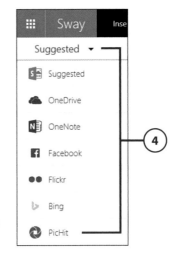

Advanced Picture Options

Advanced picture options include specifying focal points for custom cropping or selecting a showcase option to enlarge your picture. See "Formatting Text and Pictures" later in this chapter for more information.

9. Click Preview.

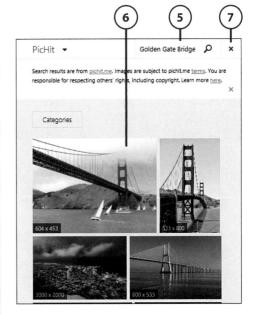

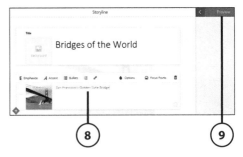

10. Sway displays a preview of your picture on the canvas.

Why Does My Picture Look Like That?

The appearance of your picture is controlled by the design you select. If you use the default design, your picture displays in a standard format, as shown in step 10. If you apply another design to your Sway, for example, your picture could display tilted with a white border. See Chapter 7 to learn more about applying designs.

San Francisco's Golden Gate Bridge

The same picture with a different design

San Francisco's Golden Gate Bridge

Another design option for this picture

San Francisco's Golden Gate Bridge

Add a Video Card

The Video Card enables you to add video from sources such as YouTube. In this example, you add a video from Que Publishing's YouTube channel.

Another Way to Add Video

Another way to add video to a Sway is to embed it. For example, you can embed video from Vimeo or Vine. See Chapter 4 for more information.

1. Click the Cards tab.

2. Drag the Video Card to the storyline.

3. Click Add a Video.

4. In the Add Content pane, click the down arrow to select a source. In this case, select YouTube.

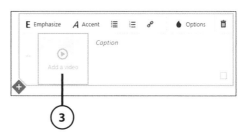

5. Enter a keyword and click the Search button. In this example, search for **Que Publishing**.

6. Drag the video to the card.

7. Click Close (x) to close the pane.

8. Enter an optional caption. See "Formatting Text and Pictures" for caption formatting options.

Showcase Your Video

Optionally, you can apply a showcase option to enlarge your video. See "Formatting Text and Pictures" later in this chapter for more information.

9. Click Preview.

10. Sway displays a preview of your video on the canvas.

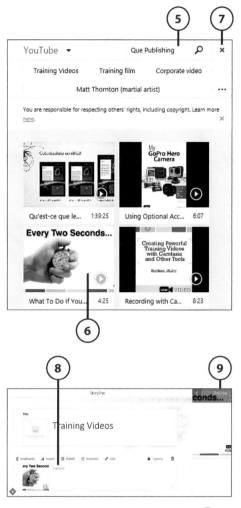

Add a Tweet Card

The Tweet Card enables you to add a Twitter tweet to your storyline. Selectively incorporating tweets in your Sway can add an interactive, social element to it.

1. Click the Cards tab.

2. Drag the Tweet Card to the storyline.

3. Click Add a Tweet.

4. In the Add Content pane, click the down arrow to select a source. In this case, select Twitter.

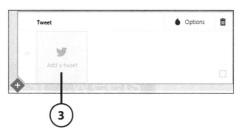

5. Enter a keyword or Twitter username and click the Search button. In this example, search for
   @QuePublishing.

6. Drag the tweet to the card.

7. Click Close (x) to close the pane.

8. The tweet displays on the
   storyline.

9. Click Preview.

10. Sway displays a preview of your
    tweet.

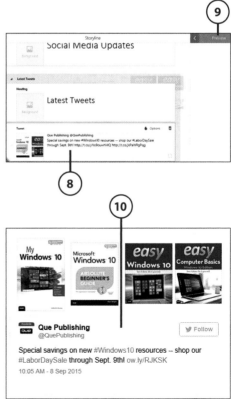

Formatting Text and Pictures

Text and picture formatting options are available on multiple cards. Your options include emphasizing and accenting selected text and inserting bulleted lists, numbered lists, and links. In addition, you can select a focus point for a picture or create a showcase with a picture or video.

>>>Go Further

EMPHASIZE AND ACCENT BUTTONS

All Sway cards that enable you to enter text include the Emphasize and Accent buttons at the top of the card.

When you first look at the Emphasize and Accent buttons, you might think that they are like the Bold and Italic buttons in other Office applications—used to apply bolding and italics to selected text. Actually, these buttons have a different effect in Sway.

The Emphasize button makes selected text stand out with one of the following options: bold, underline, color, or highlight. The Accent button makes selected text more subtle with one of the following options: italics, soft glow, shadow, or saturation.

The exact effect each button applies to your text depends on the design you select. For example, one design might display emphasized text in red using a casual font. Another might display emphasized text in blue surrounded by a white box.

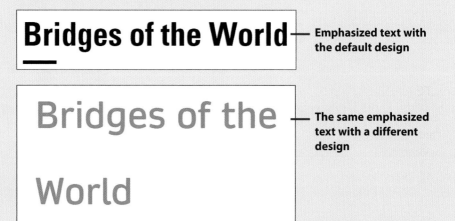

Bridges of the World — Emphasized text with the default design

Bridges of the World — The same emphasized text with a different design

In Chapter 7, you discover how to apply a new design to your Sway, changing its colors, typography, and texture. Click the Design tab on the menu to take a quick look at the available options. For now, use the Emphasize and Accent buttons to specify the text you want to emphasize or accent, but be aware that you can control the actual effect by selecting a new design.

Emphasize or Accent Text

The Emphasize button and Accent button are available on any card that contains text such as the Title Card, Heading Card, Text Card, Picture Card, or Video Card.

1. Select the text you want to format.

2. Click the Emphasize (E) button to make selected text stand out.

3. Click the Accent (A) button to make selected text more subtle.

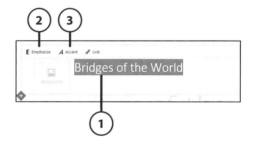

Remove Text Effects

To remove an effect, select the text and click the Emphasize button or Accent button again.

Create a Bulleted List

You can create a bulleted list on a Text Card or on the caption of a Picture Card or Video Card.

1. Select the text you want to format.

2. Click the Bullets button.

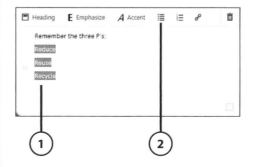

3. Sway displays the selected text as
    a bulleted list.

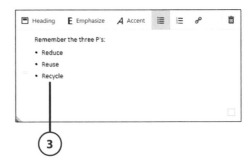

Remove a Bulleted List

To remove a bulleted list, select the text
and click the Bullets button again.

Create a Numbered List

You can create a numbered list on a Text
Card or on the caption of a Picture Card
or Video Card.

1. Select the text you want to
    format.

2. Click the Numbers button.

3. Sway displays the selected text as
    a numbered list.

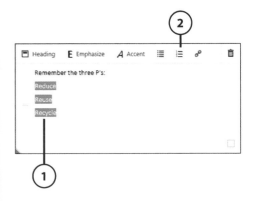

Remove a Numbered List

To remove a numbered list, select the
text and click the Numbers button
again.

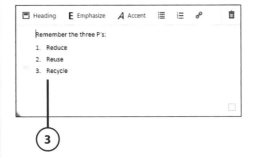

Add a Link

You can add a link to another website on any card that contains text.

1. Select the text to which you want to add the link.

2. Click the Link button.

3. Sway automatically displays your selected text in the Display Text box. Optionally, you can type in different text.

4. Enter the URL of the site you want to link to in the Web Link box.

Copy and Paste

To ensure that you enter the correct link, you can copy the URL from your browser and paste it in the Web Link box.

5. Click OK.

6. Sway underlines the link on the card.

Remove a Link

To remove a link, select the text and click the Link button again.

7. Click Preview.

8. Click the link to verify that it works.

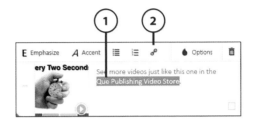

>>>Go Further
FOCUS POINTS

When you add a picture to your storyline, Sway analyzes this picture to determine the best way to crop it using its Smart Cropping algorithm. For example, Sway looks to see if there are any people in the picture or if there's a dominant object. It also evaluates the context of the picture, such as whether it's a background, a single picture, or part of a group. Based on this information, Sway crops the picture.

At times, however, you might not agree with Sway's default cropping. In these cases, you can control the cropping yourself by specifying one or more focus points. A focus point tells Sway what's important in your picture so that it can crop and reposition based on your input.

Specify Focus Points on a Picture

You can specify focus points on any card with a picture or background such as the Picture Card, Title Card, or Heading Card.

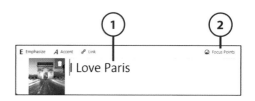

1. **Select** the picture or background on the card.

2. **Click** Focus Points.

3. **Click** one or more areas of the picture to tell Sway what to focus on.

4. The lower portion of the pane previews how your picture will appear on different sized devices.

5. **Click** Reset if you want to start over.

6. If you're satisfied with the changes, click the Close (x) button.

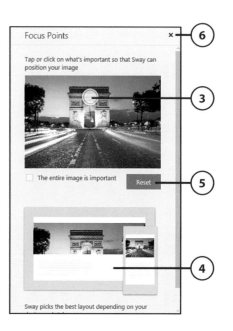

Specify Focus Points from the Canvas

If you're previewing a picture on the Sway canvas and want to specify focus points, click the picture and then click the Focus Points button to open the Focus Points pane.

Click to adjust focus points

Specify Picture and Video Showcase Options

By default, Sway displays pictures and videos at a standard size. If you want to showcase a specific picture or video, however, you can increase this size. This feature is available on the Picture Card and Video Card.

1. Select the picture or video on the card.

2. Click Options.

3. Select the showcase size you prefer.

4. Sway displays stars to let you know the showcase option of that picture (two stars for Moderate, three stars for Intense).

5. Click the Close (x) button.

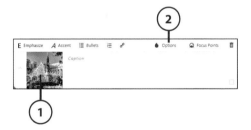

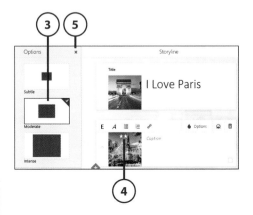

Back Up Your Sway

After adding numerous cards to the storyline, you might wonder how to back up your Sway. Although Sway saves your work automatically and stores it online, it doesn't have a specific backup function. If you've put a lot of effort into adding content to your Sway and are concerned about making a mistake that's beyond the capabilities of the Undo button, you can duplicate a Sway for safekeeping. Click the More Options (…) button on the menu, select Duplicate This Sway, and give your backup Sway a new name.

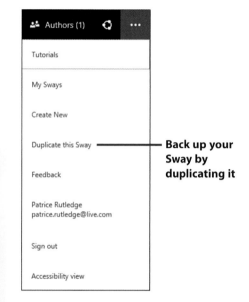

Back up your Sway by duplicating it

Welcome to the

Rainforest

Use the Automatic Card to
display a group of pictures

In this chapter, you discover how to group content—such as pictures and videos—on a single card. Specific topics in this chapter include the following:

→ Creating group cards

→ Managing group cards

Working with Group Cards

Now that you're familiar with how basic Sway cards work, it's time to move on to more complex card types. Group cards enable you to display multiple items on the same card—individually on your Sway canvas or in a slideshow or stack for a special effect. Grouping helps you present similar content in context and with some added professional polish.

Creating Group Cards

Sway offers five types of group cards:

- Automatic (standard group)

- Stack

- Comparison

- Slideshow

- Grid

Click the Cards tab to view these options on the All Cards pane along with a preview of what each option looks like.

Some cards are designed to work just with pictures, such as the Stack Card, Slideshow Card, or Comparison Card. The Grid Card enables you to display pictures or videos. The Automatic Card is the most flexible. You can use it to group pictures, videos, tweets, and more.

Add an Automatic Card

The Automatic Card displays your content in rows separated by white space. In this example, you add a group with four YouTube videos. You can also use this card to group other content, such as pictures or tweets.

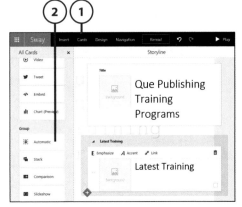

1. Click the Cards tab.

2. Drag the Automatic Card to the storyline.

3. Click Add Content.

4. In the Add Content pane, click the down arrow to select a source. In this case, select YouTube.

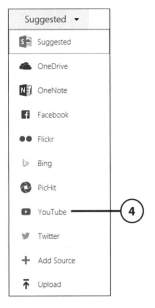

5. Enter a keyword and click the Search button. In this example, you search for **Que Publishing**.

6. Drag the videos to the card.

7. Click Close (x) to close the pane.

8. Sway displays the Automatic Card on the storyline.

9. Click Preview.

10. Sway displays a preview of your group on the canvas.

Why Does My Content Look Like That?

The appearance of your content is controlled by the design you select. For example, your content could display as shown in step 10, or your videos could have a white border, or your picture could display tiled. See Chapter 7, "Modifying a Sway," to learn more about applying designs.

Add a Stack Card

The Stack Card displays a series of pictures in a pile that viewers can click to scroll through each picture. In this example, you add a stack with five pictures from PicHit.Me.

1. Click the Cards tab.

2. Drag the Stack Card to the storyline.

3. Click Add a Picture.

4. In the Add Content pane, click the down arrow to select a source. In this case, select PicHit.

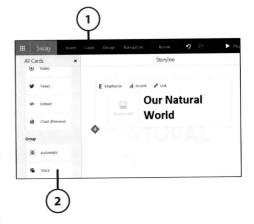

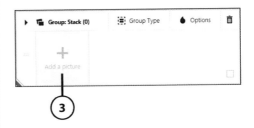

5. Enter a keyword and click the Search button. In this example, you search for **nature**.

6. Drag the pictures to the card.

7. Click Close (x) to close the pane.

8. Select the Stack Card.

9. Click Options.

Where's the Option Button?

If you have a pane open on the left side of the screen, the Options button might display as an icon without text.

10. Select your preferred picture size: Subtle (the default), Moderate, or Intense.

11. Click Preview.

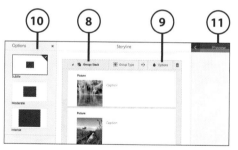

Options button without text

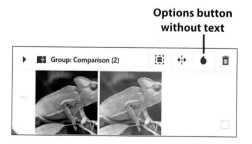

12. Sway displays a preview of your stack on the canvas. Click it to cycle through the pictures.

Add a Comparison Card

The Comparison Card enables you to compare two pictures side by side. This card works best if you want to compare a before and after or two different options. In this example, you compare two pictures stored on OneDrive.

1. Click the Cards tab.

2. Drag the Comparison Card to the storyline.

3. Click Add a Picture.

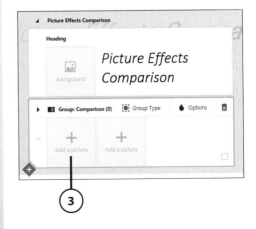

4. In the Add Content pane, click the down arrow to select a source. In this case, select OneDrive.

5. Drag the pictures to the card.

6. Click Close (x) to close the pane.

7. Select the Comparison Card.

8. Click Options.

9. Select your preferred picture size: Subtle (the default), Moderate, or Intense.

10. Click Preview.

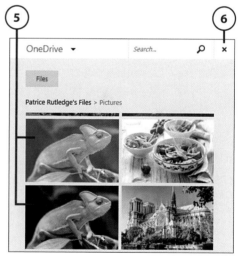

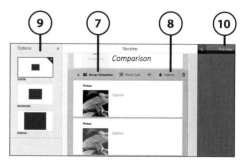

11. Sway displays a preview of your comparison.

12. Drag the slider to view either version of the picture.

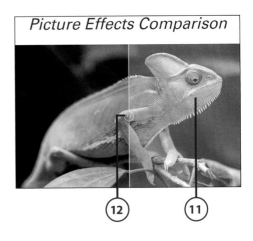

Add a Slideshow Card

The Slideshow Card enables you to create a slideshow with a series of pictures. Viewers can click the arrows on the show to scroll through each picture. In this example, you create a slideshow showcasing Lake Tahoe using four Creative Commons pictures found through Bing Image Search.

1. Click the Cards tab.

2. Drag the Slideshow Card to the storyline.

3. Click Add a Picture.

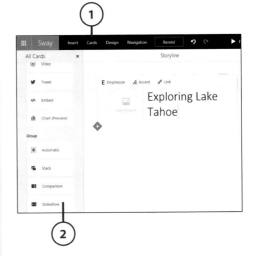

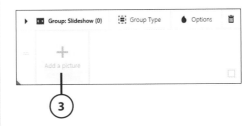

4. In the Add Content pane, click the down arrow to select a source. In this case, select Bing.

5. Enter a keyword and click the Search button. In this example, you search for **Lake Tahoe**.

6. Sway displays pictures tagged with a Creative Commons license (see Chapter 6, "Inserting Media Content," for more details about this license and its implications).

7. Drag the pictures to the card.

8. Click Close (x) to close the pane.

9. Select the Slideshow Card.

10. Click Options.

11. Select your preferred picture size: Subtle (the default), Moderate, or Intense.

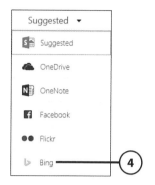

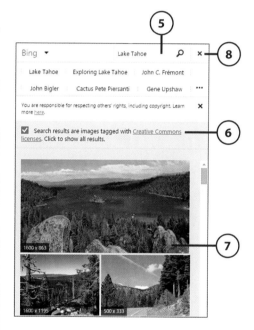

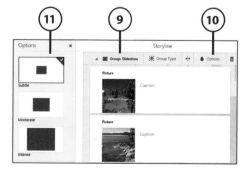

12. Select the type of slideshow you want to create: Single (the default), Thumbnail Images, or Continuous.

13. Click Preview.

14. Sway displays a preview of your slideshow on the canvas.

15. Click the arrows to scroll through the show.

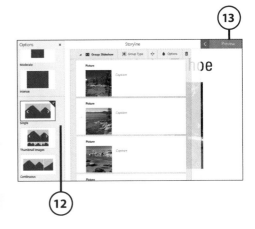

The same Sway with the thumbnails option

Add a Grid Card

The Grid Card displays your content in rows. This card is similar to the Automatic Card, but there is no white space separating the content. In this example, you add four pictures from a OneNote notebook.

1. Click the Cards tab.

2. Drag the Grid Card to the storyline.

3. Click Add Content.

4. In the Add Content pane, click the down arrow to select a source. In this case, select OneNote.

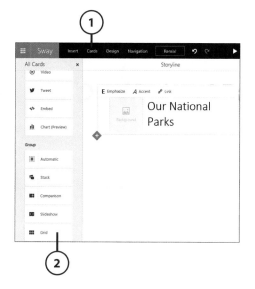

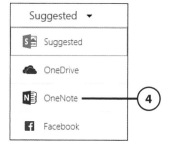

5. Drag the pictures to the card.

6. Click Close (x) to close the pane.

7. Select the Grid Card.

8. Click Options.

9. Select your preferred picture size: Subtle (the default), Moderate, or Intense.

10. Click Preview.

11. Sway displays a preview of the grid on the canvas.

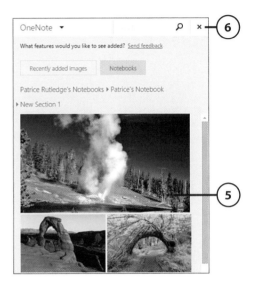

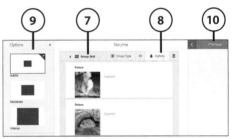

Managing Group Cards

If your group card doesn't turn out as expected, you can change its group type, ungroup it, or delete individual cards or the entire group.

Collapse a Group

By default, Sway displays each component of a group separately in an expanded format. For example, if you have four pictures in a group, they display individually. Optionally, you can collapse a group so its content displays in rows instead. If you have a lot of content in a group, or a lot of cards on your storyline, this can make it easier to view and manage your Sway.

1. Click the Collapse Group icon on the group card you want to collapse.

2. The group is collapsed.

3. Click the Expand Group icon to expand the group again.

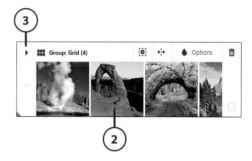

Change the Group Type

If you don't like the way a particular group card looks, you can change to a different group type without adding content again.

Change Your Design

Another way to change the appearance of your group—without switching to a new card type—is to change your design (click the Design tab to do this). A different design can have a dramatic effect on the appearance of your group, particularly with the Automatic Card. See Chapter 7 for more information.

1. Select the card whose group type you want to change.

2. Click Group Type.

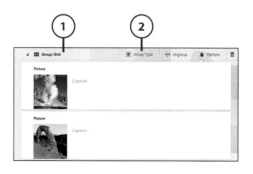

Where's the Group Type Button?

If you have a pane open on the left side of the screen, the Group Type button might display as an icon without text.

Group Type button without text

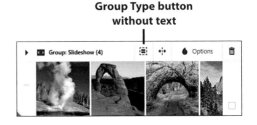

3. Select a new group type.

Available Options

Depending on the content in your group, not all group types are available. For example, if you have an Automatic Card with videos, your only option for change is to the Grid Card. If you have a Slideshow with four pictures, you can change to Automatic, Stack, or Grid Cards, but not the Comparison Card, which requires only two pictures.

4. Click Close (x) to close the pane.

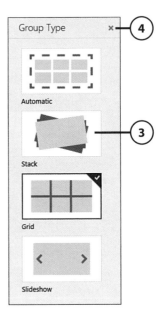

Modify Content in a Group

After you add content to a group, you might want to modify it. For example, you can:

- Add captions to individual pictures or videos and format this text by emphasizing it, accenting it, or adding bulleted or numbered lists.
- Change the order of the group content.
- Add more content to the group in a specific location, such as additional pictures or videos or related text.
- Showcase one or more pictures in the group.
- Specify a picture's focus point.
- Delete an item in the group.

1. Select the group card with content you want to modify.

2. If the group card isn't already
   expanded, click the Expand Group
   icon to expand it.

3. Sway displays the group content
   on individual cards.

4. Select the content you want to
   modify.

5. Type a caption in the text box.

6. Format selected text using buttons on the toolbar: Emphasize,
   Accent, Bullets, Numbers, or Link.

Formatting Options

See "Formatting Text and Pictures" in
Chapter 2, "Planning and Creating a
Sway," for a reminder about how these
formatting options work.

Formatting Limitations

Be aware that the formatting you apply
might not display with all group types.
For example, you can add captions to
pictures using the Automatic Card, but
these captions are hidden if you switch
to a slideshow or stack. Also, not all
formatting options are available with all
group types.

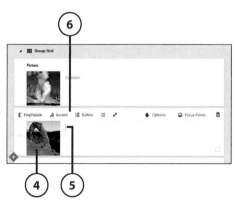

7. Click the Insert Content icon to
   insert content in the location you
   specify.

8. Click Options to specify a showcase size.

9. Click Focus Points to specify focus
   points for a picture.

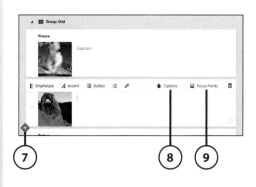

10. Click Delete (trash can icon) to delete a group item.

11. Click and drag an item to move it to a new location in the group.

12. Sway repositions the content.

13. Click the Collapse Group icon to consolidate the group content again.

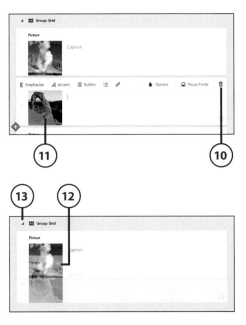

Ungroup a Group

If you decide you want to display each group item separately on the storyline, you can ungroup.

1. Select the card you want to ungroup.

2. Click Ungroup.

Where's the Ungroup Button?

If you have a pane open on the left side of the screen, the Ungroup button might display as an icon without text.

Ungroup button without text

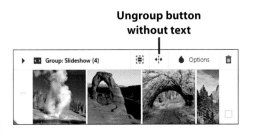

3. Sway displays each piece of the group content on a separate card.

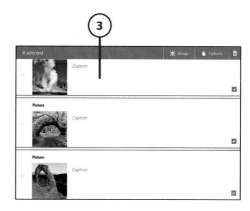

Delete a Group

If your group doesn't work out as planned, you can delete it from the storyline.

1. Select the group you want to delete.

2. Click Delete (trash can icon).

Delete a Card Within a Group

Remember that you can also delete a single card within a group by clicking its Delete icon.

Delete a card within a group

The Embed Card enables you to embed third-party content in a Sway, such as a map

In this chapter, you discover how to use the Embed Card to embed pictures, videos, audio clips, maps, infographics, and more. Specific topics in this chapter include the following:

→ Understanding the Sway embed process

→ Using the Embed Card

Embedding Content in a Sway

Another Sway card type to explore is the Embed Card. This card enables you to easily embed third-party content in your Sways. Embedding content adds a multimedia, interactive element to your Sways and avoids sending people away from your own content to external sites.

For example, you can embed videos from Vimeo or Vine, audio clips from SoundCloud or Mixcloud, maps from Google Maps, and much more.

Understanding the Sway Embed Process

Before you embed content into a Sway, take a few minutes to understand the embed process. Using the Embed Card to add content to a Sway is a little different from the cards you explored in previous chapters.

Sway Supported Sites

Sway enables you to embed content from the following supported sites:

- Channel 9
- Docs.com
- Flickr
- GeoGebra
- Giphy
- Google Maps
- Infogr.am
- Mixcloud
- Office Mix
- OneDrive (Word, Excel, PowerPoint, and PDF documents)
- Sketchfab
- SoundCloud
- Sway
- Vimeo
- Vine
- YouTube

Additional Supported Sites

Sway regularly adds support for new sites from which you can embed content. To view the most current list, click the Learn More link on an Embed Card on the storyline.

Click Learn More to view the latest list of supported sites

Three-Step Process for Embedding Content

Embedding content into a Sway is a three-step process.

1. In Sway, add the Embed Card to a storyline.

2. In the external site, copy the embed code for the content you want to embed.

3. In Sway, paste the embed code in the text box on the Embed Card.

The most challenging part of the process is often finding the embed code to copy because each supported site displays this in a different location. In general, you can find it by clicking either an Embed button or Share button near the content you want to embed.

Understand Embed Codes

An embed code is a block of HTML code, but you don't need to know anything about HTML or coding to use it—it's just a simple copy and paste action.

For example, you can copy an embed code for a Vimeo video and paste this code in the text box on an Embed Card to display the video on your Sway. You can't edit the content you embed; it essentially creates a link to this external content. This means that if the original content creator modifies the content—or deletes it—this change is reflected in your Sway.

HTML embed code ——

It's Not All Good

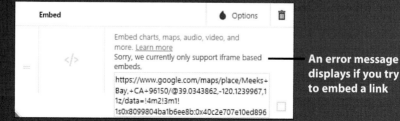

Copy the Right Code

Be sure to copy an embed code rather than a link or shortcode. Most sites offer multiple ways to share their content—embedding is often one of several options. If you paste a link or the wrong type of code in an Embed Card, Sway displays an error message.

An error message displays if you try to embed a link

Also be sure to embed content only from the sites that Sway supports. If you paste an embed code from an unsupported site, Sway displays an error message.

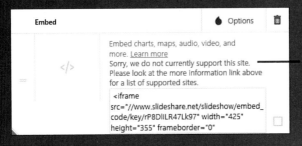

An error message displays if you try to paste an embed code from an unsupported site

>>>*Go Further*

OTHER WAYS TO EMBED CONTENT

This chapter focuses on using the Embed Card to embed content from supported sites. Because Sway is a flexible tool, it also offers other ways to embed content including the following:

- **Embed a Sway in another Sway**—You can also embed another Sway in your Sway or even create a Sway that's a collection of Sways. To discover how to do this, see "Embed a Sway in Another Sway" in Chapter 8, "Sharing a Sway."

- **Embed content from Flickr using the Picture Card or from YouTube using the Video Card**—Using the Picture Card or Video Card is the better option if you need to search for content to add to your Sway. If you know the specific Flickr picture or YouTube video you want to add, using the Embed Card is easier. See "Add a Picture Card" and "Add a Video Card" in Chapter 2, "Planning and Creating a Sway," for more information.

- **Embed content from OneDrive using the Add Content pane**—A third option is to embed content stored on OneDrive including Excel workbooks and charts, PowerPoint presentations, and Word documents. You can also embed PDFs stored on OneDrive using this method. See Chapter 6, "Inserting Media Content," for more details.

Embedding Content Using the Embed Card

The next section provides detailed examples of embedding several popular types of content into a Sway.

Embed a Map from Google Maps

If you mention a specific geographic location in a Sway, you might want to include a map of this location from Google Maps.

1. Click the Cards tab if it isn't already selected.

2. Drag the Embed Card to the storyline.

3. Sway inserts the card in the location you specified.

4. In a new browser tab, navigate to Google Maps at https://www.google.com/maps.

5. Enter the location you want to display on your map.

6. Select a match from the list.

7. Optionally, click the Search button for more matches.

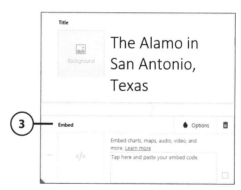

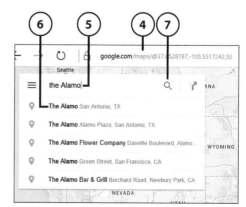

8. Google Maps displays a map based on your search term.

Find the Right Place

If the map that displays in Step 8 isn't the exact location you want, you can use your mouse to navigate to the right place or use the zoom in (+) or zoom out (-) buttons to create the map you want to embed in Sway.

9. Click the menu icon.

10. Select Share or Embed Map on the menu.

11. Click Embed Map.

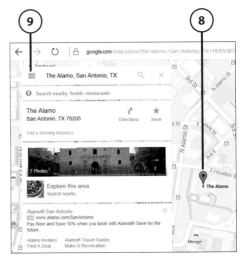

12. Select the map size you prefer. Medium is the default.

13. Click the embed code and press Ctrl + C to copy it.

14. In Sway, paste (Ctrl + V) the embed code in the text box on the Embed Card.

15. Click Preview.

16. Preview the map you embedded.

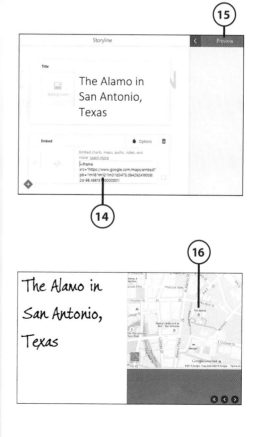

Embed an Infographic from Infogr.am

Infogr.am enables you to create online charts and infographics you can embed in a Sway.

Getting Started with Infogr.am

You need an Infogr.am account to create infographics with this web-based tool. You can find pricing information at https://infogr.am/pricing. Infogr.am offers a free 30-day trial as well as a free account that's limited to 10 infographics for noncommercial purposes.

1. Click the Cards tab if it isn't already selected.

2. Drag the Embed Card to the storyline.

3. Sway inserts the card in the location you specified.

4. In a new browser tab, navigate to Infogr.am (https://infogr.am) and open the infographic you want to embed.

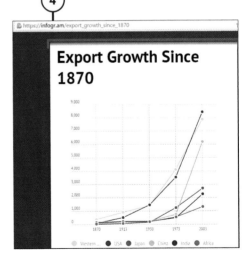

5. Scroll to the bottom of the page and click the Share button.

6. Select the Fixed tab; Sway doesn't work with the responsive version.

7. Click the embed code and press Ctrl + C to copy it.

8. In Sway, paste (Ctrl + V) the embed code in the text box on the Embed Card.

9. Click Preview.

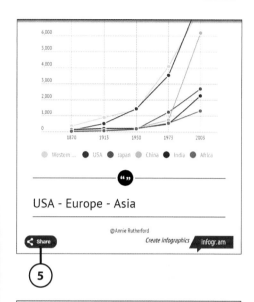

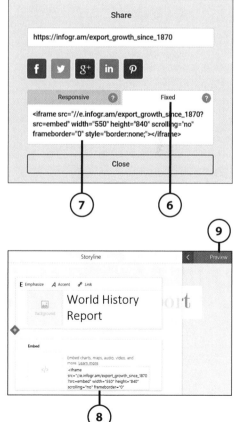

10. Preview the infographic you embedded.

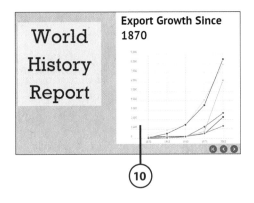

Embed a Video from Vimeo

YouTube isn't the only option for embedding video in a Sway. You can also embed Vimeo videos.

1. Click the Cards tab if it isn't already selected.

2. Drag the Embed Card to the storyline.

3. Sway inserts the card in the location you specified.

4. In a new browser tab, navigate to Vimeo (https://vimeo.com) and open the video you want to embed.

5. Click the Share button.

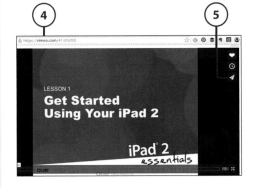

6. If you want to customize the embedded video, click Show Options.

Video Embed Options

Although the default video embed options work for most people, you can modify these settings to suit your needs. For example, you can modify the size of the video, change its colors to match your Sway design, or specify the intro content you want to include (such as a portrait, title, or byline). Other options include playing a video automatically, looping it (continuous play), or showing a text link or description below the video.

7. Modify your video's appearance using the available options if you don't like the default settings.

8. Click the embed code and press Ctrl + C to copy it.

9. In Sway, paste (Ctrl + V) the embed code in the text box on the Embed Card.

10. Click Preview.

11. Preview the video you embedded.

Embed an Audio Clip from SoundCloud

Embedding an audio clip, such as a song or podcast, from SoundCloud is another option. You don't need a SoundCloud account to embed an existing audio clip. If you want to create your own audio clips to embed, however, you must sign up for a free account on SoundCloud.

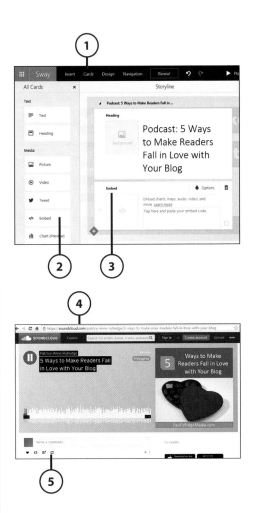

1. Click the Cards tab if it isn't already selected.

2. Drag the Embed Card to the storyline.

3. Sway inserts the card in the location you specified.

4. In a new browser tab, navigate to SoundCloud (https://soundcloud.com) and open the audio clip you want to embed.

5. Click the Share button below the clip.

6. Select the Embed tab.

7. Click the Visual Embed button to display your audio clip with a large image. This is the default setting.

8. Click the Classic Embed button to display your audio clip as a smaller rectangle.

More Options

You can customize the audio clip you want to embed if you don't like the default settings. For example, you can specify the size of a visual embed or select the player colors of a classic embed. Both embed types also enable you to play them automatically. To select these advanced options, scroll to the bottom of the clip and click the More Options link.

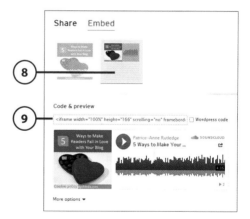

9. Click the embed code and press Ctrl + C to copy it.

10. In Sway, paste (Ctrl + V) the embed code in the text box on the Embed Card.

11. Click Preview.

12. Preview the audio clip you embedded.

Embed a Mix from Office Mix

Office Mix is a free add-in for PowerPoint that enables you to create videos with quizzes, polls, interactive apps, and more. Using an embed code, you can embed a mix in your Sway.

You don't need an Office Mix account to embed an existing mix. If you want to create your own mixes to embed, however, you must sign up for Office Mix using your Microsoft account, a work or school account, Facebook, or Google.

1. Click the Cards tab if it isn't already selected.

2. Drag the Embed Card to the storyline.

3. Sway inserts the card in the location you specified.

4. In a new browser tab, navigate to Office Mix (https://mix.office.com) and open the mix you want to embed.

5. Click the Share tab below the mix.

6. Specify your preferred size: Small (the default), Medium, or Large.

7. Click the embed code and press Ctrl + C to copy it.

8. In Sway, paste (Ctrl + V) the embed code in the text box on the Embed Card.

9. Click Preview.

10. Preview the mix you embedded.

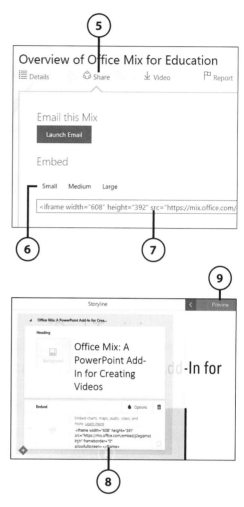

Create interactive charts directly in Sway

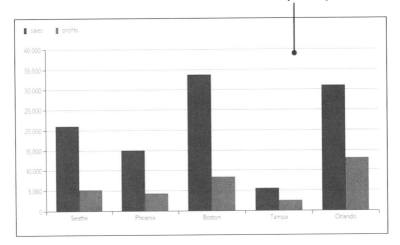

In this chapter, you explore how to create charts in Sway using its built-in interactive chart tool. Specific topics in this chapter include the following:

→ Understanding chart types and terminology

→ Adding a chart to a Sway

→ Modifying a chart

→ Previewing a chart

Working with Sway Charts

Charts enliven your Sway with visual impact and convey routine data in a way that your audience can easily understand and analyze. Sway offers a variety of chart types, including the popular column, pie, and bar charts as well as more creative options such as line and area charts.

Understanding Charts

Charts enable you to display, analyze, and compare numerical data in a graphical format. If you've created charts in other Office applications such as PowerPoint or Excel, then the Sway chart options should be familiar to you.

Understand Chart Types

Sway offers multiple chart types, some with variations to choose from. You can create the following types of charts using Sway:

- **Column**—Compare data in two or more vertical columns. This chart type works well if you want to compare categories or data across a specific time span. Sway offers two column chart types: regular or stacked. *Regular charts* display related data side by side. *Stacked charts* display data in a single stack separated by color.

  Unless you have more than one series of data, a regular chart and a stacked chart look the same. For example, if your chart lists total sales in three cities, that's one series of data (one column for each city). If your chart lists total sales in three cities for each of four quarters, you have four series of data (four columns for each city).

A regular column chart with one series of data

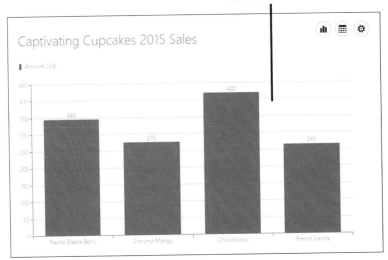

A regular column chart with
two series of data

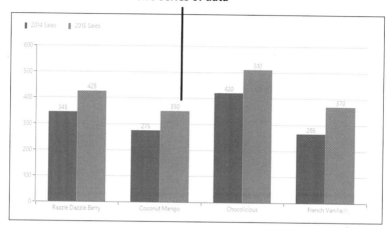

The same two series of data
in a stacked column chart

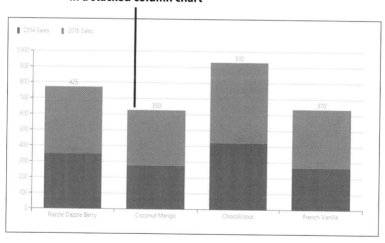

- **Bar**—Compare data in two or more horizontal bars. Like columns, you can create a regular bar chart or a stacked bar chart.

**The same data now
displayed with bars**

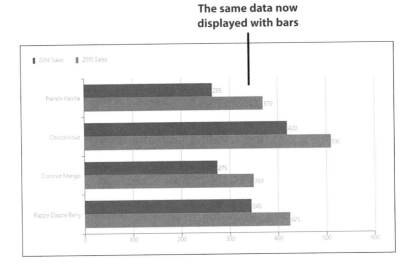

**Using the stacked
bar option**

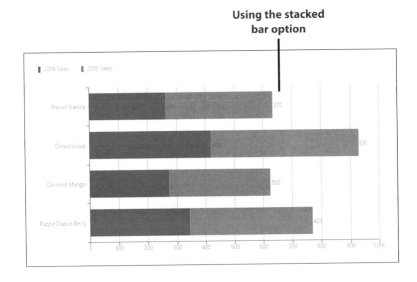

- **Line**—Display data across a line with markers for each value.

**Display and compare data
using a single line**

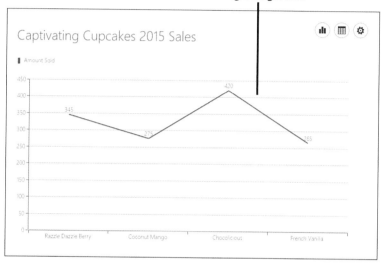

- **Pie**—Display a round pie-shaped chart showing the portions that make up a whole. Pie options include a regular pie or a donut pie. A donut pie is the same as a regular pie except that it includes a hole in the middle for a different aesthetic option.

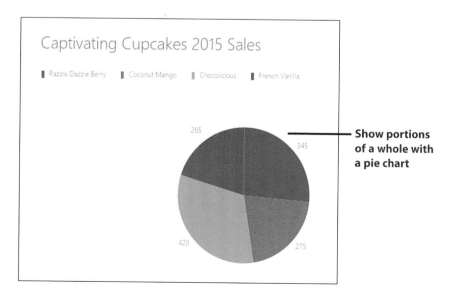

**Show portions
of a whole with
a pie chart**

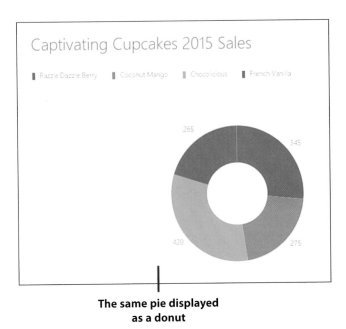

**The same pie displayed
as a donut**

- **Area**—Display value trends in a single area. This chart also offers regular or stacked options.

**An area chart is another
charting option in Sway**

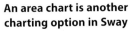

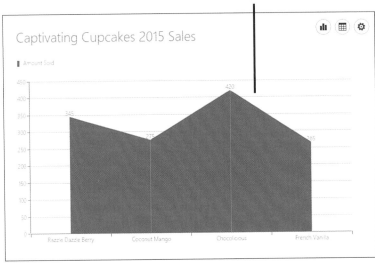

It's Not All Good

Making Smart Chart Choices

The number of available chart options can become overwhelming. To choose the right chart type, think carefully about the information you want to present and the message you want to convey with this data, and then select a chart type suited to your data.

From there, choose the variation that provides the optimal visual impact and works well with your Sway design. If you don't have a lot of experience creating charts, you might need to experiment to find just the right match.

Understand Chart Terminology

Before creating a chart, it's a good idea to learn—or refresh your memory about—basic chart terminology. Here's a list of the basic concepts you need to understand to make the most of Sway charts.

- **Axis**—A line defining the chart area. Sway charts have two axes: a vertical axis that displays data (the Y Axis) and a horizontal axis that displays categories (the X Axis).

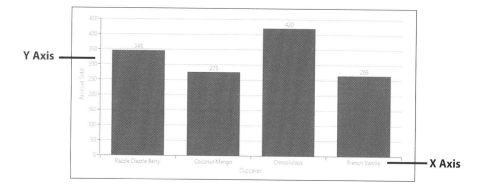

- **Worksheet**—A table with columns and rows where you can enter your chart data. A chart worksheet in Sway looks similar to an Excel worksheet, but it is smaller.

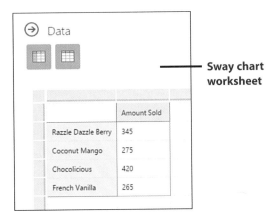

Sway chart worksheet

- **Values**—Numbers that display on a chart as columns, bars, or pie slices, for example.

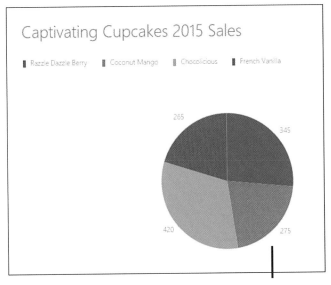

A pie chart that displays values next to each slice

- **Grid**—Lines that display across a chart that make it easier to view values and data relationships. Pie charts don't have grids.

**Gridlines make it easier to view
and analyze chart data**

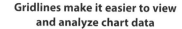

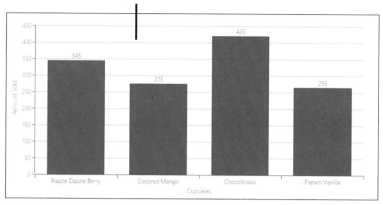

Adding a Chart to a Sway

You add a chart to a Sway using the Chart Card. In this section, you explore how to create a column chart and a pie chart.

Embed a Chart

Another way to add a chart to Sway is to embed an existing Excel chart, as described in Chapter 4, "Embedding Content in a Sway."

Add a Column Chart

You can add a regular (side-by-side) column chart or a stacked column chart using the Chart Card. In this example, you add a stacked column chart that compares units sold in three cities over three months.

1. Open the Sway in which you want to add a chart.

2. Click the Cards tab.

3. Drag the Chart Card to the storyline.

4. Click the Click Here link.

5. Sway displays the interactive chart tool on the canvas; click the tool.

6. Sway displays a sample column chart.

7. Click the Chart Type button.

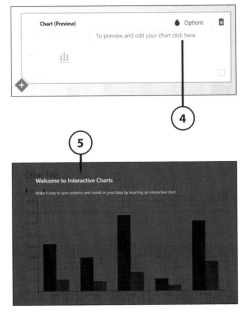

Create a Regular Chart

If you want to create a regular column chart (the default option), you can skip steps 7 through 10 when designing your own chart.

---

8. The Regular Column type is selected by default.

9. If you want to create a stacked chart, click the Stacked Column button. In this example, you're creating a stacked column chart.

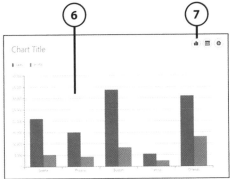

My Chart Isn't Stacked

Remember that you need more than one series of data for a stacked chart. See "Understand Chart Types" earlier in this chapter for more information.

---

10. Click the Back button.

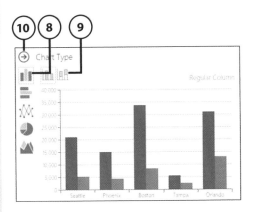

11. Click the Data button.

12. Enter your data in the chart worksheet.

What to Enter Where

Be sure to enter your descriptive text (city names and months in this example) in the row and column headers (shaded areas) and numbers in the other worksheet cells. Your chart won't display properly if you enter text in the number cells.

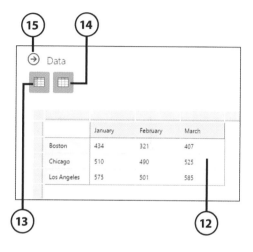

	January	February	March
Boston	434	321	407
Chicago	510	490	525
Los Angeles	575	501	585

13. Click the Toggle Column Header button if you want to hide the column headers.

14. Click the Toggle Row Header button if you want to hide the row headers.

Where Are the Buttons?

If you choose the Scrolls Horizontally navigation layout, the Toggle Column Header button and Toggle Row Header button don't appear. As a reminder, click the Navigation tab on the menu to select a layout.

Hide Column and Row Headers

If your chart doesn't need column or row headers, you can hide them from the worksheet. In this example, you need both because you have three rows (the cities) and three columns (the three months you are comparing).

15. Click the Back button.

16. Click the Settings button.

17. Enter a chart title.

18. If you want your chart to display values, click Show Values. This functions as a toggle and is set to Off by default.

Show Values

If it's important for people to know the exact value of each column, showing values is a good idea. For example, you might want to display revenue numbers or units sold.

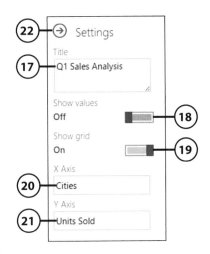

19. By default, a grid displays behind your chart. These lines make it easier for people to read your chart. If you don't want to display this, click Show Grid.

20. Type an optional name for the X Axis.

21. Type an optional name for the Y Axis.

X Axis Versus Y Axis

See "Understand Chart Terminology" earlier in this chapter for a reminder of how the X Axis and Y Axis work. In this case, you can enter "Cities" for the X Axis (categories) and "Units Sold" for the Y Axis (the data). Displaying the axes' names is optional.

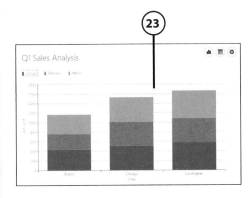

22. Click the Back button.

23. Preview your chart.

Add a Pie Chart

In this example, you create a pie chart that shows the number of students enrolled in each of five enrichment programs.

1. Open the Sway on which you want to add a chart.

2. Click the Cards tab.

3. Drag the Chart Card to the storyline.

4. Click the Click Here link.

5. Sway displays the interactive chart tool on the canvas; click the tool.

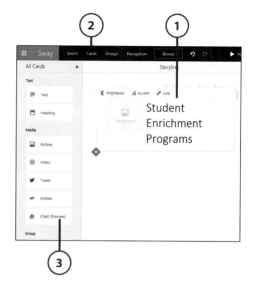

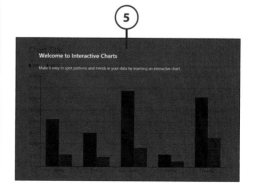

6. Click the Chart Type button.

7. Click the Pie Chart button.

8. If you want to create a donut chart, optionally click the Donut Pie button.

Donut Pie

A donut chart is a pie chart with a hole in it. It functions the same as a traditional pie chart.

9. Click the Back button.

10. Click the Data button.

11. Click the Toggle Row Header button to deselect it. You don't need this for a pie chart.

12. Enter your data in the chart worksheet.

13. Click the Back button.

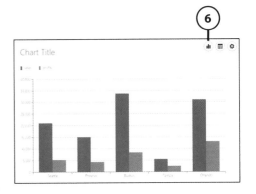

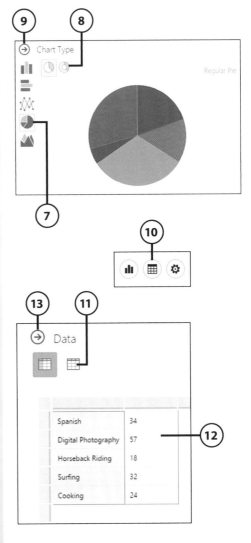

14. Click the Settings button.

15. Enter a chart title.

16. If you want your chart to display values, click Show Values. This functions as a toggle and is set to Off by default.

17. Click the Back button.

What About the Other Options?

You can ignore the Show Grid, X Axis, and Y Axis options. These don't apply to pie charts.

18. Preview your chart.

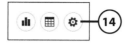

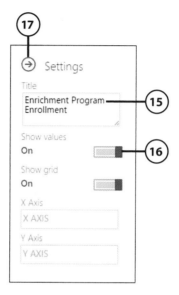

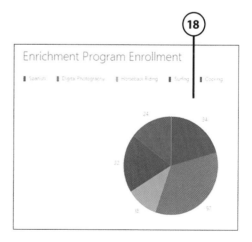

Modifying a Chart

You can modify the charts you create with the Chart Card, just as you can modify content created with other card types.

Modify Basic Chart Elements

After you create a chart, you can modify it. For example, you can switch to another chart type, edit worksheet data, or change settings.

1. Open the Sway with the chart you want to modify.

2. Click the Click Here link on the Chart Card.

3. Click the Chart Type button to switch to another chart type.

Chart Switching Limitations

Although Sway makes it easy to switch to another chart type, not all charts convert well to other formats. For example, you can switch among column, bar, and line charts with little problem. A stacked column chart, however, won't translate well as a pie chart. Before making a change, consider carefully whether the new chart type will display your data effectively.

---

4. Click Data to revise the worksheet data. See the next section, "Modify a Worksheet," for more details.

5. Click Settings to revise chart settings such as its title.

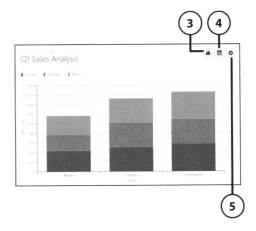

Modify a Worksheet

In addition to editing worksheet data, you can also add and delete rows and columns.

1. Open the Sway with the chart you want to modify.

2. Click the Click Here link on the Chart Card.

3. Click the Data button.

4. Select a column.

5. Click the Insert Left button to insert a new column to the left of the selected column.

6. Click the Insert Right button to insert a new column to the right of the selected column.

7. Click the Delete Columns button to delete the selected column.

8. Select a row.

9. Click the Insert Above button to insert a new row above the selected row.

10. Click the Insert Below button to insert a new row below the selected row.

11. Click the Delete Rows button to delete the selected row.

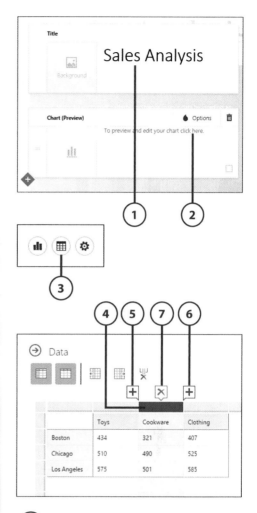

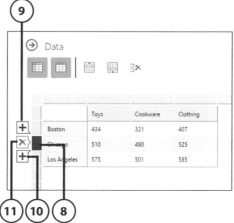

Specify Chart Showcase Options

By default, Sway displays charts at a standard size. If you want to showcase a specific chart, however, you can increase this size.

1. Select the chart you want to showcase.

2. Click Options.

3. Select the showcase size you prefer: Subtle (the default), Moderate, or Intense.

4. Click the Close (x) button.

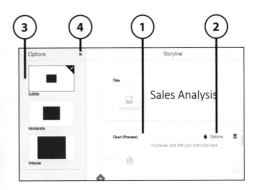

Previewing a Chart

Although you can preview a chart as you create it, it's a good idea to preview the final chart before sharing. Depending on the chart type you select and the data you enter, Sway might enable viewers to interact with the chart and select only specific data to see.

Preview a Chart

Preview your chart to see it the way your audience will.

1. Open the Sway with the chart you want to preview.

2. Click Preview.

3. Preview the way other people will see your Sway.

4. Pause over a column to view more information.

5. Click to view only specific data. In this example, you view only data for January.

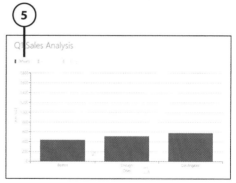

The Add Content pane is smart:
it suggests content based on your
storyline text, such as titles and headings

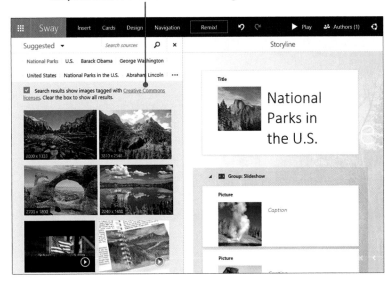

In this chapter, you discover how to use the Add Content pane to quickly add pictures, videos, tweets, documents, and more to your Sways. Specific topics in this chapter include the following:

→ Exploring the Add Content pane

→ Adding content from the Add Content pane

→ Adding content from OneDrive

→ Uploading content from your computer

→ Suggesting new content sources

Inserting Media Content

You should be familiar with the Add Content pane from the previous chapters. In this chapter, you explore this powerful tool in more depth.

In addition to dragging and dropping content from popular sources such as Bing and YouTube, you can use this pane to import or embed Office files (Word, Excel, and PowerPoint) and PDFs, or even upload files from your own computer.

Exploring the Add Content Pane

Using the Add Content pane, your focus is on selecting content to add to your Sway—either your own content or Creative Commons-licensed content on the Web. When you find what you're looking for, just drag it to the storyline and Sway adds the appropriate card type.

The Add Content pane enables you to add content from the following sources:

- OneDrive
- OneNote
- Facebook
- Flickr

- Bing
- PicHit
- YouTube
- Twitter

Add Content pane sources

Suggest More Sources

Because Sway is a new app, Microsoft is continually adding features to it. You can have your say in the future direction of Sway by suggesting new content sources such as Instagram, Pinterest, Dropbox, Google Drive, or another preferred source. See "Suggesting New Content Sources" later in this chapter to learn how to do this.

Picture, Image, or Photo?

The Add Content pane often uses different terminology to refer to the same type of visual content: picture, photo, and image. That's because different apps use different terms to describe this same content. In this chapter, I use the preferred terminology of each app. For example, you add images from Bing and OneNote, and photos from Facebook, Flickr, and PicHit.Me, to a Sway Picture Card.

The Add Content pane makes it even easier to find great content to add to your Sway by suggesting relevant content based on the text in your storyline. This built-in intelligence enables you to discover quality content you might not have otherwise found. See "Add Content from Suggested Sources" later in this chapter.

>>>*Go Further*

UNDERSTANDING COPYRIGHT AND CREATIVE COMMONS LICENSES

When you create a Sway, you must have the right to use the content you add to it, such as pictures and videos. If you create the content yourself, you obviously have the right to use it in your Sway. But what about that great image you found using Bing Image Search on the Add Content pane?

When you select Bing as a source on this pane, Sway displays images tagged with a Creative Commons license. This is a public copyright license that gives you the right to use or share the creative works of another person.

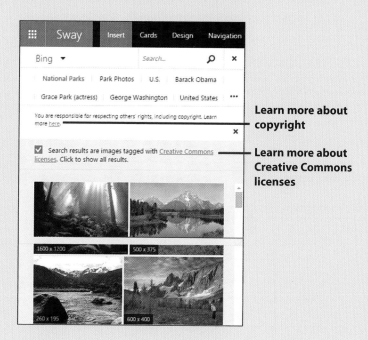

Learn more about copyright

Learn more about Creative Commons licenses

For example, a photographer might assign a Creative Commons license to her images, enabling you to find them via Bing Image Search and freely add them to your Sway in exchange for attribution.

A Creative Commons license that requires attribution means that you must give credit to the content creator. In the previous example, you can use the photographer's images if you give her credit in your Sway. For an example of attribution in a published Sway, view the sample Sway that's included in your account, EXAMPLE: Fabrikam Workshop, which includes photo credits at the end. You can also find this example at https://sway.com/9-hgFciW_RTs6UkM.

Although a Creative Commons license is most common with images, you also must verify your right to include other types of content. In addition, Bing Image Search is only one example of a source that suggests Creative Commons-licensed content. You can also find these images through Flickr or PicHit.Me via the Add Content pane.

Because legal issues surrounding the use of content in your Sways is beyond the scope of this book, it's important that you verify that you have the legal rights to any third-party content you want to use even if it does display on the Add Content pane. This is particularly important if you plan to share your Sway publicly on the Web.

Here are two resources to help you understand this topic:

- http://www.microsoft.com/en-us/legal/Copyright/Default.aspx

- http://creativecommons.org/licenses

Adding Content from the Add Content Pane

The next section provides detailed examples of adding content using the Add Content pane.

Add Content from Suggested Sources

Based on your existing storyline text, Sway suggests additional content you might want to add. When you choose this option, Sway searches its sources to find related content. For example, it might display images from Bing Image Search, tweets from Twitter, or videos from YouTube.

1. Click the Insert tab.

2. If this is the first time you're using the Add Content pane, the Suggested source is selected by default. If not, select it from the drop-down list.

3. Sway displays related content by topic; click the option that's the best match.

What's That?

Although the suggested content usually relates directly to the Sway you're creating, sometimes it includes unrelated suggestions. This is particularly true if your Sway contains limited text or if the content can be interpreted in more than one way. For example, a Sway titled "National Parks in the U.S." returned search results related to national parks as well as results related to the U.S. in general, and people with the last name Parks.

---

4. Optionally, enter your own search terms and click the Search button.

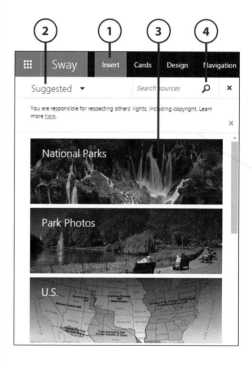

5. Sway displays individual content suggestions, such as pictures, videos, tweets.

6. If you want to see more options, click another search tag.

7. If you want to return to the previous screen, click the … button.

8. Drag the content you want to the storyline.

9. Click Close (x) to close the pane.

10. Sway adds the content to the appropriate card type (in this example, it's a Picture Card).

Add Multiple Content

You can add multiple items from the Add Content pane to your storyline at the same time. Select each item you want to add, such as multiple images, and click the Add button at the top of the pane to add each image to a separate Picture Card on the storyline.

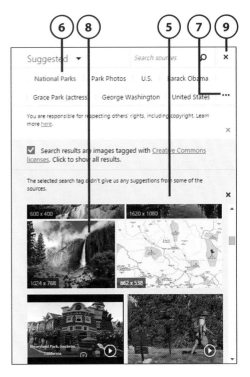

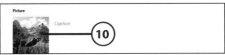

Select multiple images   Add button

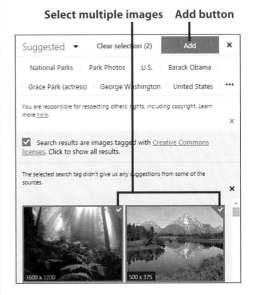

Add Content from OneNote

If you store visual content in OneNote, you can easily add these images to Sway. This includes standard images such as JPG and PNG files, screen clips you create using the OneNote Clipper, or content you scan using Office Lens.

Office Lens

Office Lens is a free document-scanning app available for iPhone, Windows Phone, and Android phones that enables your smartphone to function as a scanner. Using Office Lens, you can photograph receipts, business cards, paper documents, whiteboards, blackboards, menus, and more, and store these scanned images in OneNote. To install this app, search for it in your phone's store such as the Google Play Store, iTunes Store, or Windows Phone Store.

1. Click the Insert tab.

2. Select OneNote from the drop-down list.

3. By default, Sway displays recently added images.

Where's My Content?

Be aware that Sway searches the content of OneNote notebooks stored on OneDrive. If you have other OneNote notebooks, you won't see their content here. Also remember that Sway currently searches only for images in OneNote, not other content.

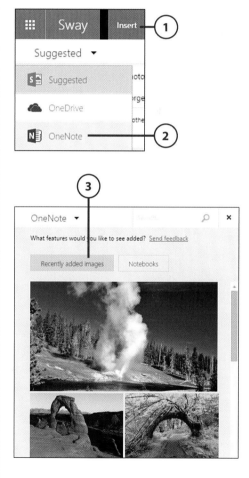

4. If the image you want doesn't display in the list, click the Notebooks button to search for images in other notebooks.

5. Drag the image you want to the storyline.

6. Click Close (x) to close the pane.

7. Sway adds the image to a new Picture Card on the storyline.

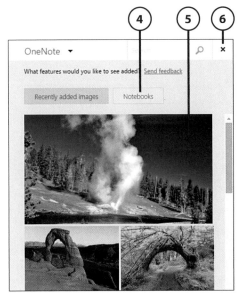

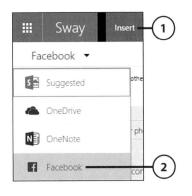

Add Content from Facebook

If you want to insert photos and videos from Facebook in Sway, you can connect Facebook to your Microsoft account.

Profile Versus Page

Be aware that this option connects your personal Facebook profile, not any Facebook pages that you manage. In addition, you can only add photos and videos. You can't currently embed Facebook posts.

1. Click the Insert tab.

2. Select Facebook from the drop-down list.

3. Click the Connect Facebook button.

Logged In to Facebook?

If you aren't already logged in to Facebook, you're prompted to do so.

4. Click the Connect Facebook button to confirm you want to connect Facebook to your Microsoft account.

5. Facebook informs you how Microsoft uses your data.

What Can Sway Do with My Facebook Content?

Connecting Facebook with your Microsoft account gives Microsoft apps such as Sway access to your Facebook public profile, photos, and videos. In this case, you're giving Sway the right to insert Facebook photos and videos in your storyline. It doesn't, however, give any Microsoft app the right to post to your Facebook timeline.

6. Click Okay to confirm.

7. Click the Insert tab again.

8. Select Facebook from the drop-down list.

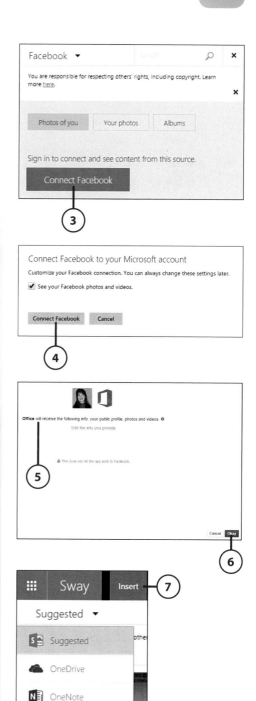

9. Click Photos of You to display photos that include you—your own photos or photos from other people in which you're tagged.

10. Click Your Photos to display your timeline photos.

11. Click Albums to search for a photo in a particular album.

12. Drag the photo you want to the storyline.

13. Click Close (x) to close the pane.

14. Sway adds the photo to a new Picture Card on the storyline.

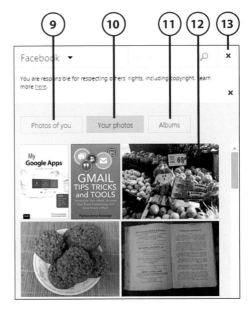

Add Content from Flickr

You can add photos from your Flickr photostream or albums to a Sway. Optionally, you can search for Creative Commons-licensed photos from other users.

In this example, you search Flickr for third-party content and verify the Creative Commons license of the photo you want to use. See "Understanding Copyright and Creative Commons Licenses" earlier in this chapter for a reminder about how to select appropriate content for your Sway.

Embed Content from Flickr

Another option is to embed a photo from Flickr by pasting its embed code on an Embed Card on your Sway storyline. This option works best if you know the exact photo you want to use. If you want to search for content, using the Add Content pane is easier. See Chapter 4, "Embedding Content in a Sway," for more details.

1. Click the Insert tab.

2. Select Flickr from the drop-down list.

3. Click Connect Flickr if you want to connect to your own Flickr account.

4. If you want to search Flickr for third-party content, enter a search term and click the Search button. In this example, you search for pictures related to **Que Publishing**.

5. Select the photo you want to add to your Sway.

6. Click this photo's link to open it in Flickr.

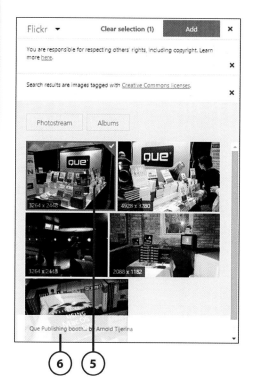

7. View the photo's Creative Commons license icons.

8. Click the Some Rights Reserved link for details on this license.

9. This particular photo is available for you to use with attribution (you give the photographer credit) and if your use is non-commercial. These are common requirements for Creative Commons licenses.

10. Close any external tabs when you're finished reviewing them.

11. Click the Sway tab to return to your storyline.

12. In Sway, drag the photo to the storyline.

13. Click Close (x) to close the pane.

14. Sway adds the photo to a new Picture Card on the storyline.

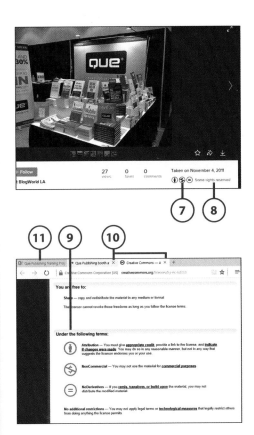

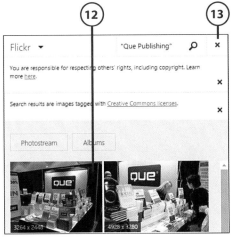

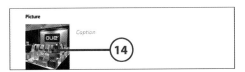

Add Content from Bing

Adding images you discover using Bing Image Search is another possibility. This option enables you to search the Web for images tagged with a Creative Commons license and add them directly to your Sway storyline. See "Understanding Copyright and Creative Commons Licenses" earlier in this chapter for a reminder about how to select appropriate content for your Sway.

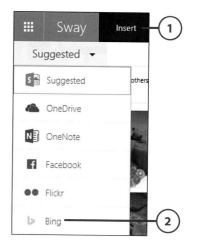

1. Click the Insert tab.

2. Select Bing from the drop-down list.

3. Sway displays related content by topic; select the option that's the best match.

4. If you want to search for images, enter your keywords and click the Search button.

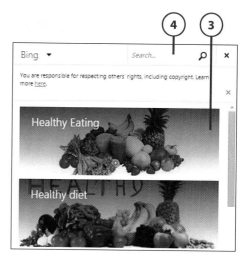

5. Optionally, select an image and click the link at the bottom of the pane to view the image's source. This often includes image license details.

6. To view more options, click another search tag.

7. To return to the previous screen, click the … button.

8. Drag the image you want to the storyline.

9. Click Close (x) to close the pane.

10. Sway adds the image to a new Picture Card.

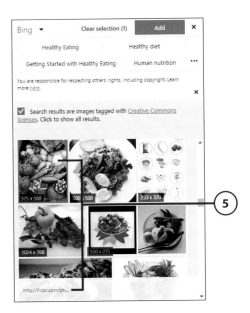

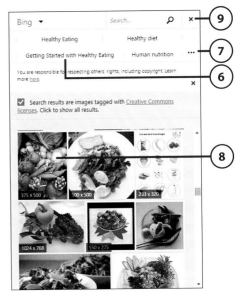

Add Content from PicHit

Yet another source of visual content for
Sway is PicHit.Me, shortened to PicHit in
Sway. This site is a global photo market
and Microsoft partner that makes millions of photos available to Microsoft
users. You can search the PicHit library
by category such as Business & Industry
or Cities & Places. Another option is to
search by keyword.

1. Click the Insert tab.

2. Select PicHit from the drop-down
   list.

3. Sway displays related content by
   category; select the one that's the
   best match for your needs.

4. Optionally, enter your own
   keywords and click the Search
   button.

5. Drag the photo you want to the storyline.

6. Click Close (x) to close the pane.

7. Sway adds the photo to a new Picture Card on the storyline.

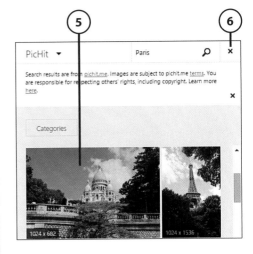

Add Content from YouTube

You can enliven your Sway with video content from YouTube.

Embed Content from YouTube

Another option is to embed a video from YouTube by pasting its embed code on an Embed Card on your Sway storyline. This option works best if you know the exact video you want to use. If you want to search for videos, using the Add Content pane is easier. See Chapter 4 for more details.

1. Click the Insert tab.

2. Select YouTube from the drop-down list.

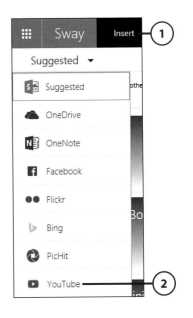

3. Sway displays videos related to your storyline content.

4. If you want to see more options, click another search tag.

5. Optionally, enter your own keywords and click the Search button.

6. Drag the video you want to the storyline.

7. Click Close (x) to close the pane.

8. Sway adds the video to a new Video Card on the storyline.

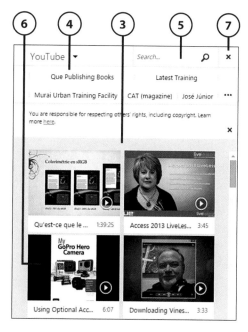

Add Content from Twitter

Incorporating tweets into your storyline adds a social element to it. Sway searches for tweets that match the text on your storyline, but you can also search by keyword or username.

1. Click the Insert tab.

2. Select Twitter from the drop-down list.

3. Sway displays related tweets.

4. If you want to see more options, click another search tag.

5. Optionally, enter your own keywords and click the Search button.

Search by Username

Another option is to search for tweets by username such as **@quepublishing** or **@patricerutledge**. This displays tweets from that username as well as tweets mentioning that username.

6. Drag the tweet you want to the storyline.

7. Click Close (x) to close the pane.

8. Sway adds the tweet to a new Tweet Card on the storyline.

Adding Content from OneDrive

From the Add Content pane, you can add documents stored on OneDrive to your storyline. This includes the option to either import or embed Word, PowerPoint, and PDF documents. You can also embed Excel workbooks, including those with graphs and charts, or insert pictures stored on OneDrive. If you sign in to Sway with an Office 365 school or work account, you can access your content on OneDrive for Business.

>>>Go Further

IMPORTING VERSUS EMBEDDING

When you add a Word document, PowerPoint presentation, or PDF to your Sway, you have the option of importing or embedding the content. There is a big difference between the two, both in terms of how you can use the content and how it displays in your Sway.

- **Import**—Display the file content on multiple cards in the storyline. For example, if you import a Word document with text and pictures that uses the Title and Heading 1 styles, Sway breaks this content into sections using multiple cards such as Heading, Text, and Picture Cards. You can then edit the content on these cards to create a custom Sway.

- **Embed**—Insert the file as is and enable viewers to scroll through the content in its native format. Using this option, Sway adds a single Embed Card to the storyline with an embed code (a small block of HTML code) that links to the original content. When you embed content, you can't edit it. For example, you could embed a PowerPoint presentation and enable your Sway viewers to scroll through it slide by slide.

The remainder of this section provides step-by-step examples that show you how to import and embed content from OneDrive.

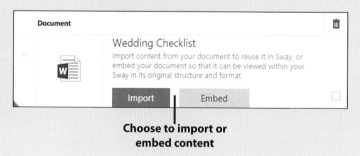

Choose to import or embed content

Embed Codes and Other Embedding Options

For a reminder about embed codes and additional ways to embed content in Sway, see Chapter 4.

It's Not All Good

Importing Limitations

Before importing a Word document, PowerPoint presentation, or PDF, consider carefully whether Sway can easily separate its content into cards on a storyline. For example, a file with basic text and pictures usually imports without difficulty. A file with complex formatting isn't as likely to work well. In this case, embedding is a better option.

Add a Word Document from OneDrive

You can import or embed a Word document in Sway.

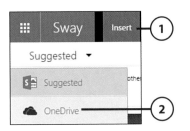

Create a New Sway from a Word Document

Another option is to create a new Sway by importing a Word document. See "Create a New Sway by Importing Content" in Chapter 1, "Getting Started with Office Sway." If you want to import or embed a Word document in an existing Sway, use the steps described in this section.

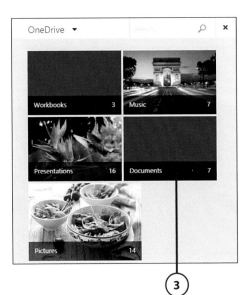

1. Click the Insert tab.

2. Select OneDrive from the drop-down list.

3. Select the folder that contains the Word document you want to add.

4. Drag the document to the storyline.

5. Click Close (x) to close the pane.

6. If you want to import this document, click the Import button. (If you want to embed, skip to step 10.)

7. Sway displays the document content on multiple cards.

8. Click Preview.

9. Preview the imported document on the canvas.

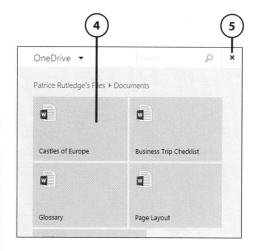

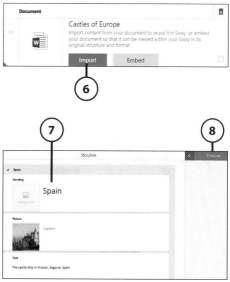

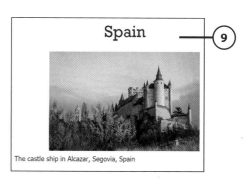

The castle ship in Alcazar, Segovia, Spain

10. If you want to embed this document, click the Embed button. Be aware that if you chose to import in step 6, this option is no longer available.

11. Sway adds the document using an embed code on a single Embed Card.

12. Click Preview.

13. Preview the embedded document on the canvas.

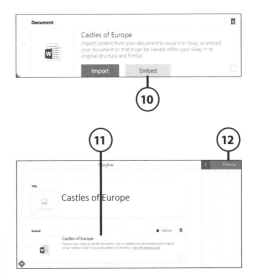

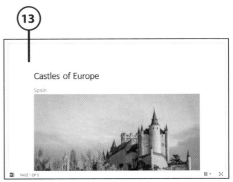

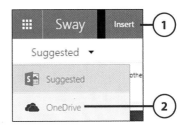

Add a PowerPoint Presentation from OneDrive

You can import or embed a PowerPoint presentation in Sway.

1. Click the Insert tab.

2. Select OneDrive from the drop-down list.

Create a New Sway from a PowerPoint Presentation

Another option is to create a new Sway by importing a PowerPoint presentation. See "Create a New Sway by Importing Content" in Chapter 1. If you want to import or embed a presentation in an existing Sway, use the steps described in this section.

3. Select the folder that contains the PowerPoint presentation you want to add.

4. Drag the presentation to the storyline.

5. Click Close (x) to close the pane.

6. If you want to import this presentation, click the Import button. (If you want to embed, skip to step 10.)

7. Sway displays the presentation content on multiple cards.

8. Click Preview.

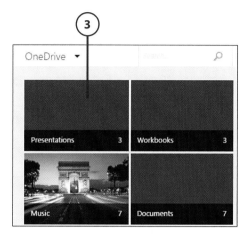

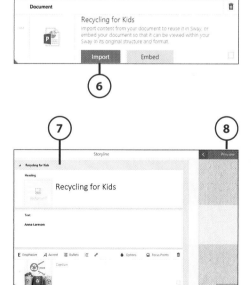

9. Preview the imported presentation on the canvas.

10. If you want to embed this presentation, click the Embed button. Be aware that if you chose to import in step 6, this option is no longer available.

11. Sway adds the presentation using an embed code on a single Embed Card.

12. Click Preview.

13. Click View.

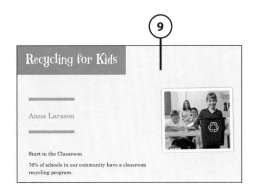

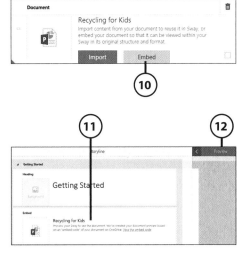

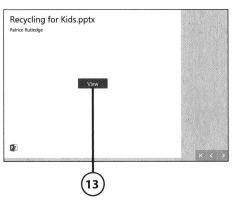

14. Preview the embedded presentation on the canvas.

Add an Excel Workbook from OneDrive

You can embed an Excel workbook in Sway, including a workbook that contains a chart or graph. There is no option to import an Excel workbook because it would be difficult to display this data on separate Sway Cards.

1. Click the Insert tab.

2. Select OneDrive from the drop-down list.

3. Select the folder that contains the Excel workbook you want to add.

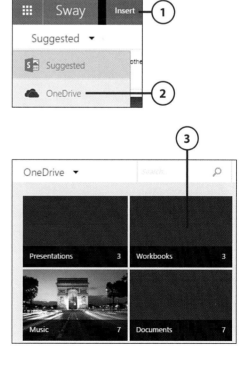

4. Drag the workbook to the storyline.

5. Click Close (x) to close the pane.

6. Sway adds the workbook using an embed code on a single Embed Card.

7. Click Preview.

8. Click View.

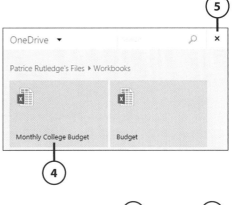

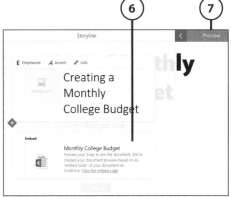

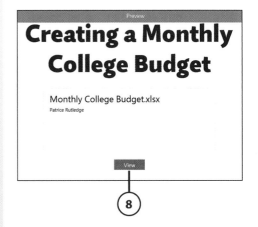

9. Preview the embedded workbook on the canvas.

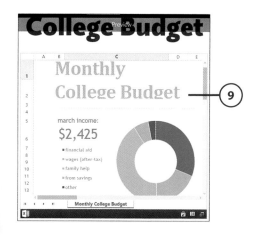

Add a PDF from OneDrive

You can import or embed a PDF document in Sway.

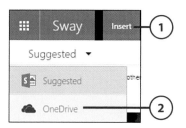

Create a New Sway from a PDF

Another option is to create a new Sway by importing a PDF. See "Create a New Sway by Importing Content" in Chapter 1. If you want to import or embed a PDF in an existing Sway, use the steps described in this section.

1. Click the Insert tab.

2. Select OneDrive from the drop-down list.

3. Select the folder that contains the PDF you want to add.

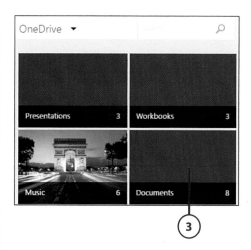

4. Drag the PDF to the storyline.

5. Click Close (x) to close the pane.

6. If you want to import this PDF, click the Import button. (If you want to embed, skip to step 10.)

7. Sway displays the PDF content on multiple cards.

8. Click Preview.

9. Preview the imported PDF content on the canvas.

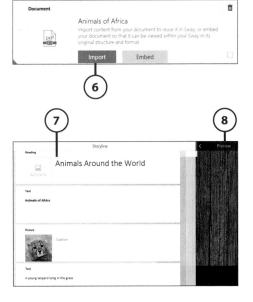

10. If you want to embed this PDF, click the Embed button. Be aware that if you chose to import in step 6, this option is no longer available.

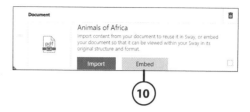

11. Sway adds the PDF using an embed code on a single Embed Card.

12. Click Preview.

13. Click View.

14. Preview the embedded PDF on the canvas.

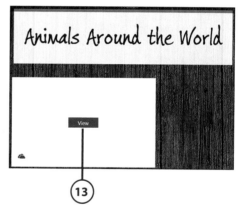

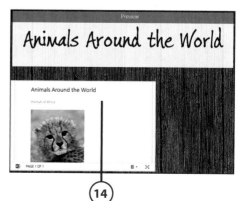

Uploading Content from Your Computer

You can upload Office files (Word, Excel, and PowerPoint), PDFs, and images (JPG, PNG, TIFF, and so forth) from your computer to Sway. Uploading a file is very similar to adding a file from OneDrive, only the source location is different.

When you upload, you have the choice of importing or embedding Word documents, PowerPoint presentations, and PDFs. See "Importing Versus Embedding" earlier in this chapter for more details.

Upload a File from Your Computer

In this example, you upload and embed a PowerPoint presentation.

1. Click the Insert tab.

2. Select Upload from the drop-down list.

3. In the Open dialog box, select the file you want to upload.

Where's My File?
The Open dialog box displays only files that you can upload to Sway. It doesn't display all files on your computer.

4. Click Open.

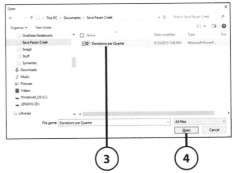

5. Click the Embed button.

6. Sway displays the document as an embed code on a single Embed Card.

7. Click Preview.

8. Click View.

9. Preview the embedded document on the canvas.

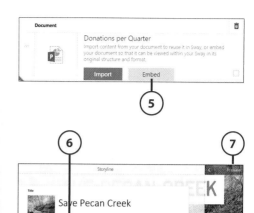

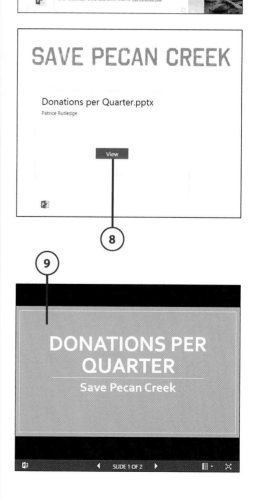

Suggesting New Content Sources

If you would like to add content from a source that's not yet available on the Add Content pane, you can suggest it to the Sway team at Microsoft. For example, you might want to suggest Instagram, Pinterest, Dropbox, Google Drive, or another source you're interested in.

Suggest New Content Sources

Let the Sway team know which content sources you want them to add.

1. Click the Insert tab.

2. Select Add Source from the drop-down list.

3. Specify the content sources you want Sway to add.

4. Click the Send button to send your suggestions.

Not Now

If you decide you don't want to submit your feedback, click the Not Now button to return to your storyline.

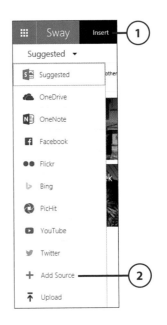

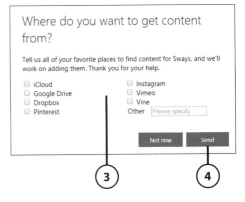

You're in control of your
Sway's design

In this chapter, you discover how to modify a Sway—its content, layout, design, styles, and colors. Specific topics in this chapter include the following:

→ Opening, renaming, duplicating, and deleting Sways

→ Moving and deleting cards on the storyline

→ Modifying Sway design

→ Previewing a Sway

Modifying a Sway

After you create a Sway, you'll probably want to modify it. Fortunately, Sway makes it easy to do this with simple one-click and drag-and-drop options. If you're more interested in design elements, Sway enables you to apply a coordinated design set—or customize it with the exact colors, fonts, and styles you want.

Working with a Sway

You can open, edit, rearrange, duplicate, rename, or delete a Sway.

Open a Sway

When you're logged in to Sway, you can easily open a Sway you already created.

1. If you aren't already on the My Sways page, click Sway.

2. On the My Sways page, click the Sway you want to open.

3. The Sway opens, ready for you to edit.

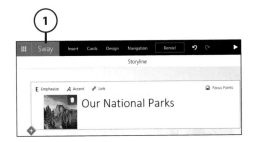

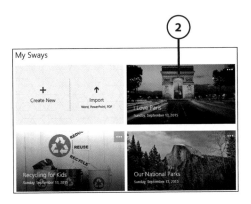

All Sways

If you're working on one or more shared Sways that someone else created, the My Sways page is renamed to All Sways. The steps to open a Sway are identical regardless of the page name. The All Sways page, however, does have an additional drop-down menu that you can click to specify whether you want to view only your own Sways or only Sways shared with you. If you have a lot of Sways, this can make it easier to find the exact Sway you want to open.

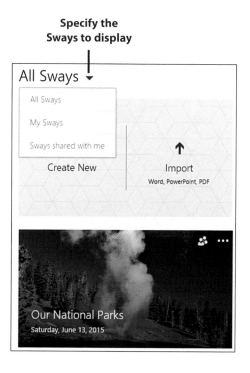

Specify the Sways to display

Rename a Sway

If you don't like a Sway's original name, you can rename it.

1. Open the Sway you want to rename.

2. Select the title text.

3. Replace the selected title with your new title.

E Emphasize A Accent ∂ Link   Focus Points

Our National Parks

②

③

Title

National Parks in the U.S.

Duplicate a Sway

Duplicating a Sway is a useful feature. You can duplicate a Sway you plan to edit to create a backup—just in case you make mistakes that go beyond the capabilities of the Undo button. You can also duplicate a Sway if you want to reuse content or design elements in a new Sway, saving you time and effort.

Duplicate a Shared Sway

Duplicating a Sway you shared with others is another good idea. The more people who have edit access to a Sway, the easier it is for someone to accidentally make a mistake. This is particularly true for new Sway users. Creating a duplicate that only *you* have access to helps you recover quickly from a Sway-sharing disaster. Be sure to create a new duplicate after your Sway team performs any extensive edits or adds new content.

1. Open the Sway you want to duplicate.

2. Click the More Options (…) button.

3. Select Duplicate This Sway.

4. Enter a new name for the duplicate Sway.

5. Click the Duplicate button.

6. Click the Go to My Sways button to return to the My Sways page.

7. Click the Edit It Now button to open the storyline for the duplicate Sway.

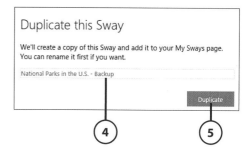

Another Way to Duplicate a Sway

You can also duplicate a Sway from the My Sways page. Click the More Options (…) button on the Sway you want to duplicate, and then click the Duplicate button to open the Duplicate This Sway dialog box shown in step 4.

More Options button

Duplicate button

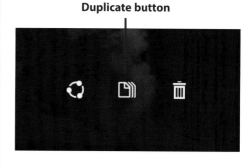

Delete a Sway

If you decide you no longer need a Sway, you can delete it.

1. On the My Sways page, click the More Options (…) button on the Sway you want to delete.

2. Click the Delete button.

Where's the Delete Button?

The Delete button doesn't appear on shared Sways because you can't delete a Sway that was shared with you. You can only delete Sways you created yourself.

3. Click Confirm Delete to permanently delete this Sway.

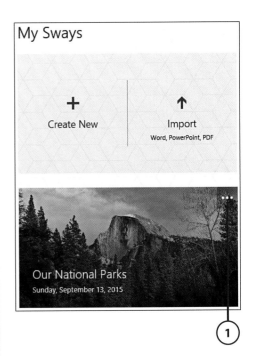

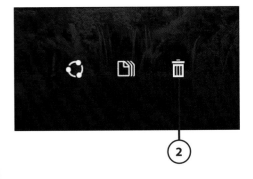

It's Not All Good

Deletion Is Permanent

Consider carefully before deleting a Sway. Sway offers no backup option other than creating a duplicate, so if you make a mistake, you can't undo your deletion.

Modifying Sway Content

When you open an existing Sway, you can modify content on the storyline just like when you created it. You can add, move, and delete cards; edit card content; and add and delete external media. You can also modify the Sway layout.

Editing card content is very similar to creating it. See Chapters 2 through 5 for a reminder of how to work with each card type.

Move a Card on the Storyline

You can rearrange your storyline by moving its cards.

1. In an open Sway, select the card you want to move.

2. Drag it to a new location on the storyline using the repositioning handle.

3. The card displays in its new location.

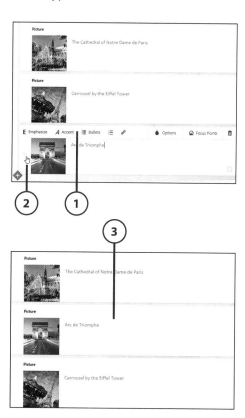

Move a Section

You can also move an entire section to another location on the storyline. Being able to quickly move multiple cards is one of the big advantages of using heading sections on your storyline.

Delete a Card or Section

If you make a mistake or no longer need specific content on your storyline, you can delete it. Sway enables you to delete individual cards or entire sections in a single click.

1. In an open Sway, select the card or section you want to delete.

2. Click the Delete (trash can) icon.

Oops!

When you click the Delete icon, Sway deletes your content without asking for a confirmation. If you delete something accidentally, click the Undo button on the menu to restore it.

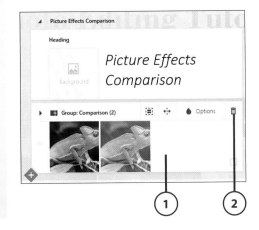

Modifying Sway Design

When you create a Sway, a default design set is applied, which includes a coordinated collection of colors, typography, and textures. This affects all the elements of your Sway: text, boxes, lines, pictures, videos, and backgrounds.

In this section, you view some examples of how applying a different design set can change the appearance of your Sway dramatically—in only seconds.

The design set you select controls the appearance of the title text

The same title with a different design set

**Some design sets display pictures
without special formatting**

**The same pictures tilted
with a white border**

**Elaborate borders and backgrounds
are part of selected design sets**

>>>Go Further

WHAT'S A DESIGN SET?

A design set includes the following elements, which you can customize:

- **Color inspiration**—A picture or curated set of colors that controls the color palettes available for a specific Sway. You can use the inspiration curated by Sway or select a picture from your Sway itself as your color inspiration. If you choose the latter option, the color palette displays colors found in the selected picture.

- **Color palettes**—A collection of coordinated colors based on your color inspiration. Sway applies these colors to text, shapes, boxes, and backgrounds.

- **Font choices**—A coordinated pair of fonts designed for titles, headings, captions, and regular text.

- **Animation emphasis**—The level of animation and movement in your Sway. There are three options available: subtle, moderate, or intense.

You can control all of these elements when you customize a selected design set. See "Customize a Design Set" later in this chapter for more information.

It's Not All Good

Don't Go Overboard with Design

Although Sway makes it fun and easy to try new designs, remember that usability is the most important factor when creating a Sway. Be sure to select a design set that matches the tone of your topic and enhances your content rather than distracts from it.

Apply a New Design Set

If you don't like your Sway's default design, you can apply a new design set.

1. Open the Sway whose design you want to modify.

2. Click the Design tab.

3. View the current design set.

4. Use the arrows to scroll through the available design sets.

5. Select a new design set.

6. Click Preview.

7. Preview your design.

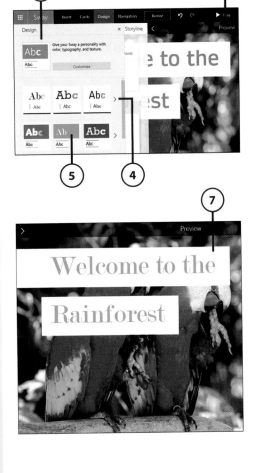

Customize a Design Set

If your selected design set isn't quite right, you can customize it to suit your needs. For example, you can customize the color inspiration, color palette, fonts, and animation emphasis.

1. Open the Sway whose design you want to customize.

2. Click the Design tab.

3. Select the design set you want to customize.

4. Click the Customize button.

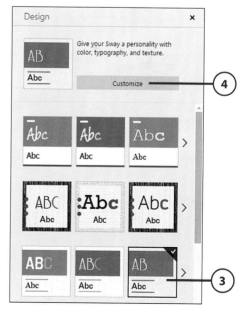

5. Select your color inspiration. See "What's a Design Set?" earlier in this chapter for a reminder of the available design set options.

6. Select a color palette.

7. Select a font pair from the Font Choices drop-down list.

8. Select an animation emphasis: subtle, moderate, or intense.

9. Click Preview.

10. Preview your customized design.

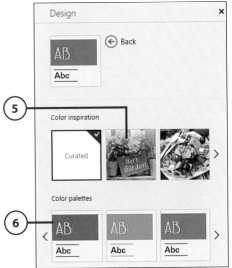

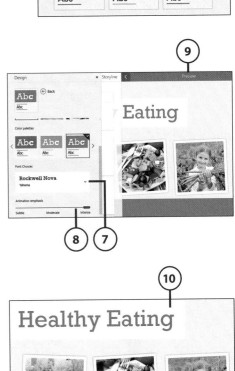

Modify Your Sway's Design Automatically with Remix!

If you're adventurous, try Remix! to change the design of your Sway automatically with a single click.

1. Open the Sway whose design you want to remix.

2. Click Remix!

3. Sway applies a random design.

4. Click Remix! again.

5. Sway applies another design.

6. Continue clicking Remix! until you find a design you like.

Escape Plan

After using Remix!, you can return to your previous design by clicking the Undo button. If you apply multiple remixes, however, it can be difficult to find your way back to your original look. If you plan to try out numerous design options with Remix!, it's a good idea to click the Design tab and note which design set is applied before you start remixing. That way, you can return to this design if none of the remixes suits your needs. Optionally, you can create a duplicate of a Sway you plan to remix.

Discover Your Favorite Remix

When you find a remix you like, you might want to know which design set it is so that you can use it again with other Sways. Click the Design tab and view the current design to discover which set Sway applied.

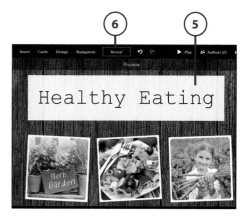

Switch to Another Layout

If you don't like the layout originally applied to your Sway, you can change it. For example, you might want to switch from a vertical layout (scroll down the page) to a horizontal layout (slideshow) or a layout that's optimized for presentation (each card on a separate screen). See "Working with Navigational Layouts" in Chapter 2, "Planning and Creating a Sway," for more information about Sway layouts.

1. Open the Sway whose layout you want to modify.

2. Click the Navigation tab.

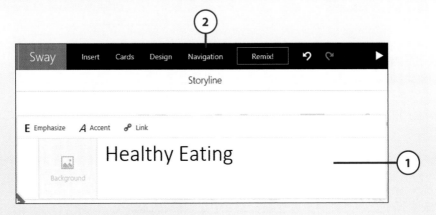

3. Select the layout you want to apply.

4. Click Close (x).

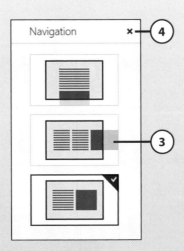

Sway using a vertical layout

Scroll to navigate

The same Sway using a horizontal layout

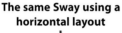

Click buttons to navigate

Sway optimized for
presentation

Click buttons
to navigate

Each card displays on a
separate screen

Previewing a Sway

Before you share your Sway with others, you should preview it. When previewing, verify that:

- Your Sway is easy to navigate and read.

- Nothing is missing or in the wrong place.

- The spelling and grammar are correct.

- The design complements your content and doesn't distract from it.

If you notice any problems or errors, fix them before sharing.

Preview a Sway

You can preview your Sway as you create it to see what changes you might need to make.

1. Open the Sway you want to preview.

2. Click Preview.

3. Preview your Sway.

4. Click Open Storyline to return to the storyline.

Play a Sway

In addition to previewing a Sway, you can play it. Play adds animation to your Sway and shows you how your audience will see it.

1. Open the Sway you want to play.

2. Click Play.

3. Your Sway begins to play.

4. Use navigation buttons to scroll through the Sway (only with the horizontal layout and optimized for presentation layout).

5. Click Edit to stop playing and return to the preview window.

6. Click Share This Sway Socially to display sharing options. See Chapter 8, "Sharing a Sway," for more information.

7. Click More Options (…) to display the More Options menu.

How Do Others See My Sway?

Although playing a Sway is very similar to the way others see your Sway, there are a few differences. For example, viewers can't edit your Sway and their choices on the More Options menu are limited (they can't duplicate or access your My Sways page).

8. Scroll to the end or bottom of the Sway to view the Made with Sway section.

9. Click Get Started to create a new Sway.

10. Share on social sites such as Facebook or Twitter.

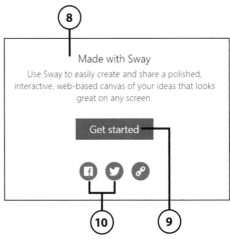

Use Accessibility View

Sway offers an accessibility view that makes it easier for people to see and navigate your content. With this view, Sway content displays in high contrast for easier reading. Sway content is also made available for a screen reader.

1. Open the Sway you want to see with accessibility view.

2. Click the More Options (…) button.

3. Select Accessibility View from the menu.

4. A new browser tab opens, displaying the Sway in accessibility view.

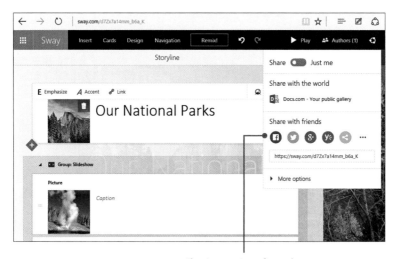

Sharing options from the
Share menu button

In this chapter, you discover how to share your Sway—with the world or just a few people. Specific topics in this chapter include the following:

→ Specifying sharing options

→ Sharing your Sway on Docs.com

→ Sharing on social sites or via email

→ Sharing with links

→ Sharing from the My Sways page

→ Managing shared Sways

→ Embedding a Sway

Sharing a Sway

Because Sways are meant to be shared, Sway offers numerous options for sharing. To start, you can specify whether you want to share your Sway or keep it to yourself (for now). When you're ready to share, you can do so on popular social sites such as Facebook and Twitter, on Microsoft's public sharing site Docs.com, with a view-only link, or via email.

You can also share an edit link with others, enabling them to collaborate with you on a Sway. You remain in control of sharing and can revoke sharing rights at any time.

Finally, you can also embed a Sway on a website or blog or even on another Sway (creating a Sway within a Sway).

Specifying Sharing Options

Sway offers two sharing options that determine who can—and can't—view each Sway you create. These are

- **Share**—Your Sway is available for public viewing on Docs.com, for sharing on social sites, or for sharing via a link.

- **Just Me**—Your Sway is private and you're the only person who can see it. This setting is best for a Sway that you're currently designing and you don't want anyone to see yet.

Default Sharing Setting

When you create a new Sway, the default sharing setting is Share. Optionally, you can change this to Just Me until your Sway is ready for its debut.

Specify Who Can See a Sway

It's a good practice to check your sharing settings when you first create a Sway as well as when you finish it.

1. Click the Share button on the menu.

2. Select Share to share your Sway with others (default setting).

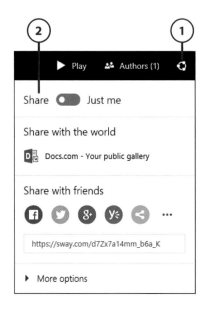

3. Click Just Me to make this Sway private and accessible only to you.

Update the Just Me Option
If you select the Just Me setting for in-progress Sways, be sure to change this setting to Share when you are ready to share.

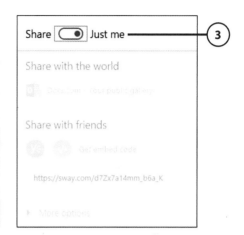

Sharing Your Sway on Docs.com

Publishing your Sway on Docs.com is one of Sway's many sharing options. Docs.com is Microsoft's file-sharing site, where you can upload and share Sways as well as Word documents, Excel workbooks, PowerPoint presentations, Office Mix video presentations, and PDFs.

It's Not All Good

Consider Your Sharing Options Carefully

Anything you share on Docs.com is public. It's accessible by anyone who uses Docs.com, is available in search engine results, and can be shared by others on social sites.

This is good if you're looking for broad exposure for your Sway or the project it represents. It isn't good if your Sway is meant for a small group of people or you haven't completed it yet.

Create an Account on Docs.com

To get started sharing on Docs.com, you need a Microsoft account. This is the same account you use to sign in to Sway.

1. Verify that you're signed in to your Microsoft account. If you're currently signed in to Sway, you're signed in to your account.

2. Navigate to https://docs.com in a new browser tab. Docs.com detects your country and language automatically and modifies the URL, such as https://docs.com/en-us.

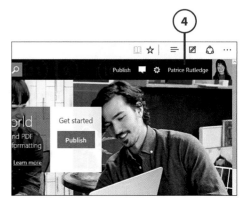

3. Click Sign In.

4. Click your name.

5. Click the Create My Account button.

6. Click Edit Background to add, edit, or remove a background image.

7. Click Edit to add a link to your website and a bio of up to 1,000 characters.

8. Click New Sway to create a new Sway.

Docs.com and Sway

You can create a new Sway from within Docs.com or share an existing Sway on this site, as described in the next section. You can also use a Sway as your Docs.com background.

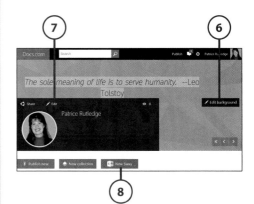

Share a Sway on Docs.com

If you want to share your Sway with the world, you can do so on Docs.com.

1. Click the Share button.

2. Select the Share option if it isn't already selected.

3. Click Docs.com—Your Public Gallery.

4. Optionally, click the Here link to learn more about copyright.

Understand Copyright Rules Before Publishing

Before publishing your Sway on Docs.com, verify whether you have the right to share its content and images, especially if you didn't create them yourself. See "Understanding Copyright and Creative Commons Licenses" in Chapter 6, "Inserting Media Content," for more information.

5. Click the Publish button.

6. View the publish notification that displays. When this dialog box disappears, your Sway is published on Docs.com.

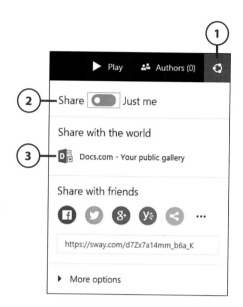

Manage Your Sway on Docs.com

When your Sway is published on Docs.com, you can view it on that site as well as manage its properties and appearance.

1. Click the Share button.

2. Click the Manage on Docs.com button.

3. View your Sway on Docs.com.

4. Add this Sway to a Docs.com collection, a group of related content.

5. View full screen.

6. Click Details to manage this Sway's properties and presence on Docs.com.

7. Click the Edit This Document button.

8. Add your author name.

9. Enter a description.

10. Select any additional options.

Other Options

Optionally, you can also customize your background image, add tags to enhance searchability, disable comments, or specify Creative Commons licenses on this page.

11. Click Done.

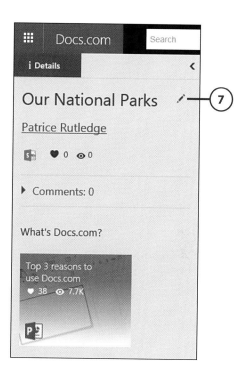

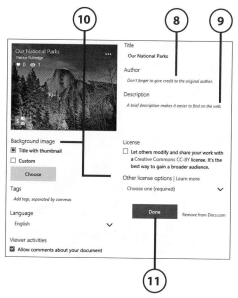

Unpublish a Sway on Docs.com

If you decide you no longer want to make your Sway available to the public on Docs.com, you can unpublish it.

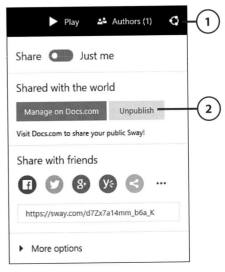

1. In your Sway, click the Share button.

2. Click the Unpublish button.

3. Click the Unpublish button.

4. View the unpublish notification that displays. When this dialog box disappears, your Sway is unpublished on Docs.com.

Another Way to Remove Your Sway from Docs.com

You can also remove your Sway directly in Docs.com on its details page. Click the Remove from Docs.com link next to the Done button (described in step 11 of the previous section).

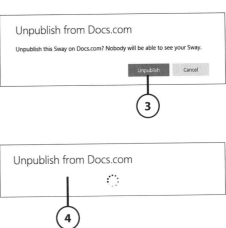

Getting Social with Sway

If you want public exposure for your Sway, you can share it on many popular social sites. Sway enables you to share directly to Facebook, Twitter, Google+, and Yammer. Using the ShareThis social-sharing tool, you can share to dozens of other popular sites, as well as share via email.

Share a Sway on Facebook

Sharing on Facebook is easy with Sway.

1. Click the Share button.

2. Select the Share option if it isn't already selected.

3. Click the Share to Facebook button.

Where's the Share to Facebook Button?

The Share to Facebook button isn't available unless you select the Share option in step 2.

4. Specify where you want to share this Sway: on your own timeline, on a friend's timeline, in a group, on a page you manage, or in a private message. In this example, you share on your own timeline.

Log In to Facebook

If you aren't already logged in to Facebook, Sway prompts you to do so before you can share.

5. Add a comment in the Say Something About This box.

6. Specify who can see your post: the public, just your friends, or a custom audience.

7. Click the Share Link button to post on Facebook.

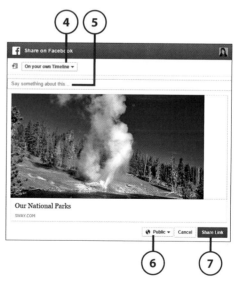

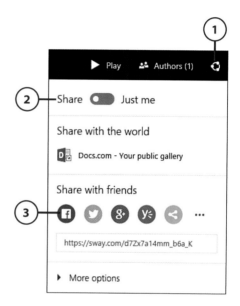

Share a Sway on Twitter

You can also share your Sway on Twitter.

1. Click the Share button.

2. Select the Share option if it isn't already selected.

3. Click the Share to Twitter button.

Where's the Share to Twitter Button?

The Share to Twitter button isn't available unless you select the Share option in step 2.

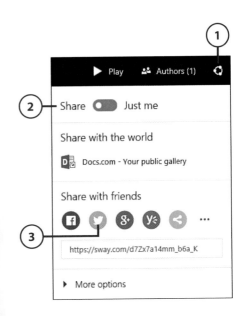

4. A window opens with a suggested tweet that you can modify.

Log In to Twitter

If you aren't already logged in to Twitter, Sway prompts you to do so before you can share.

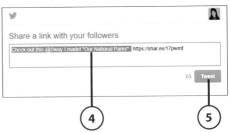

@Sway

If you retain the @sway mention, the Sway team might see your tweet. You might also want to consider following @sway for the latest news on Sway and Sway-related tips.

5. Click the Tweet button to share your tweet on Twitter.

Schedule Your Tweet

If you use a social media scheduling tool such as Buffer or Hootsuite, you can schedule your tweet rather than share it immediately.

Share on Other Social Sites

Although you can share on certain sites directly from Sway, you can also share on these sites using the ShareThis social-sharing tool. ShareThis enables you to share on dozens of other popular sites as well, including LinkedIn, Digg, Evernote, Buffer, Pinterest, and many more. In this example, you share your Sway on Pinterest but the process is similar with other sites.

1. Click the Share button.

2. Select the Share option if it isn't already selected.

3. Click the Share This Sway Using Other Social Services button.

Where's the Button?

The Share This Sway Using Other Social Services button isn't available unless you select the Share option in step 2.

4. Click the More (…) button to view the available social sites.

Shortcut

If you want to share via Facebook, Twitter, or LinkedIn, add a comment, click the appropriate icon in the lower-left corner of the dialog box, and then click the Share button. Otherwise, click the More button to view dozens of additional options.

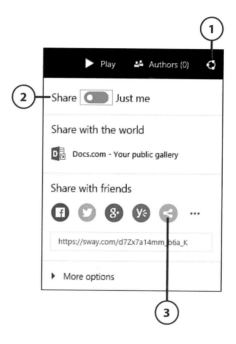

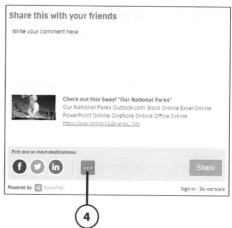

5. Select the site where you want to share this Sway. In this example, select Pinterest. If you aren't signed in, you're prompted to do so.

6. Add a pin description.

7. Select the board where you want to share your Sway.

8. Click the Pin It button.

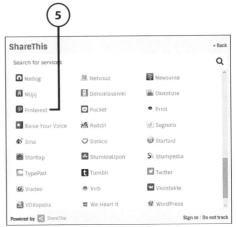

Share via Email

ShareThis also enables you to share a Sway via email. You can share using Gmail, Yahoo!, Outlook.com, or another email client. In this example, you share using Outlook.com.

1. Click the Share button.

2. Select the Share option if it isn't already selected.

3. Click the Share This Sway Using Other Social Services button.

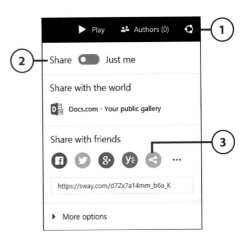

4. Click the More (…) button to view more options.

5. Select Email.

6. Select the email client you use. In this case, select Outlook.

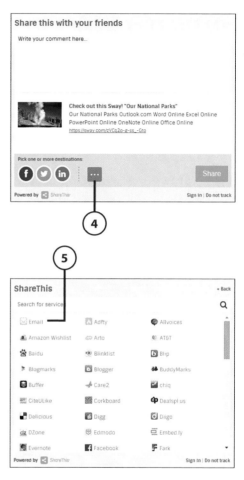

7. A new message opens with a link to your Sway. You can modify this message with your own text.

8. Enter the email address of the person to whom you want to send this Sway.

9. Click Send.

Sharing with Links

Links make it easy for other people to view your Sways. You can enable others to edit a Sway you created or just view it.

Share a View Link

Let others view your Sway by sharing a link. They don't need a Sway account to view your content; they can view it on the Web.

1. Click the Share button.

2. Select the Share option if it isn't already selected.

3. Copy (Ctrl+C) the link in the Share with Friends box.

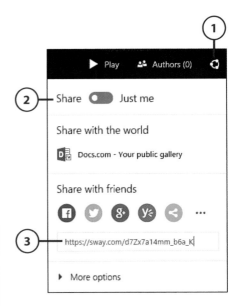

Next Steps

From here, you can share this link with the people you want to view your Sway. For example, you can paste (Ctrl+V) the link in an email message or post online. To view your Sway as others who have the link will see it, log out of Sway and paste the link in a new browser window.

Shared link   **Share this Sway**   **More options**

View your Sway as others with your link will see it

Share an Edit Link

Sharing an edit link with others enables them to modify your Sway in their own Sway account, creating a collaborative environment for developing Sways.

1. Click the Authors button.

2. Copy (Ctrl+C) the link in the Share an Edit Link box.

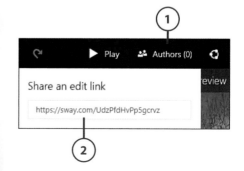

Next Steps

From here, you can share this link with the people you want to edit your Sway. For example, you can paste (Ctrl+V) the link in an email message or post on a secure site. See "Edit a Sway Someone Shared with You" later in this chapter to discover how others can edit a Sway you shared.

Sharing a Sway from the My Sways Page

Sharing a Sway directly from the My Sways page is yet another option.

All Sways Page

If you're already editing a shared Sway, the My Sways page is renamed to the All Sways page. Sharing from this page works the same regardless of the name change.

Share from the My Sways Page

The My Sways page lets you share Sways from one central location.

1. Click Sway.

2. Click the More Options (...) button on the Sway you want to share.

3. Click the Share button.

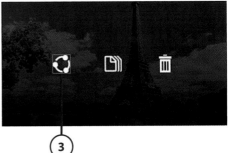

4. Click the Share to Facebook button to share on Facebook.

5. Click the Share to Twitter button to share on Twitter.

6. Click the Share by Link button to share a view link.

7. Click the Add Author button to share an edit link.

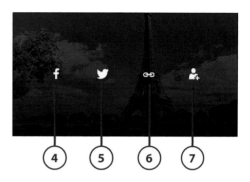

How to Share

Previous sections of this chapter cover how to share via Facebook, Twitter, view links, or edit links. The My Sways page just offers another way to access these same features.

Managing Shared Sways

It's easy to edit, view, and remove yourself from Sways shared with you. If you share a Sway with others, you can revoke this access.

Edit a Sway Someone Shared with You

If someone sends you an edit link to a Sway, you can make changes to it using your own Sway account.

1. While logged in to Sway, open the link shared with you in your browser.

2. Click the Edit button.

View Without Editing

If you want to view a Sway before accepting the offer to edit it, click the View Only button.

3. The Sway opens and is available for you to edit.

4. Click the Show Authors button to view a list of people who can edit this Sway.

My Link Doesn't Work

If you can't access a Sway link someone provided you, the sender might have deleted the Sway, selected a sharing setting of Just Me, or revoked access to the Sway (see "Stop Sharing a Sway" later in this chapter). Contact the sender for more details or to request a new link.

View Sways Shared with You

When you start editing a shared Sway, the My Sways page is renamed to All Sways. From this page, you can identify which Sways are yours and which are Sways shared with you.

1. Click Sway.

2. The Show Authors button identifies shared Sways.

3. Click the All Sways down arrow.

4. Click Sways Shared with Me.

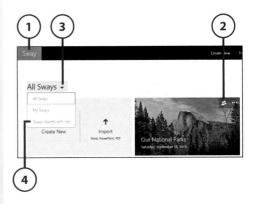

View Your Own Sways

You can also display only your own Sways by selecting My Sways from the drop-down list.

5. View shared Sways on the Sways Shared with Me page.

Stop Sharing a Sway

If you decide you no longer want anyone to see a Sway you've shared, you can stop sharing. When you do this, no one can view or edit your Sway even if they have a link you previously shared. In addition, if you shared this Sway on Docs.com, it's removed.

1. Click the Share button.

2. Click More Options.

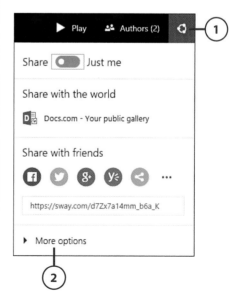

3. Click Stop Sharing.

4. Click the Stop Sharing button.

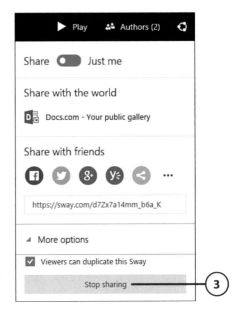

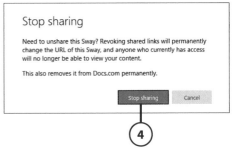

Remove Yourself from a Shared Sway

You can remove a Sway someone shared with you from your Sway account if you no longer need access to it.

1. Click Sway.

2. Click the Show Authors icon on the shared Sway you want to remove.

3. Click the Remove Me button.

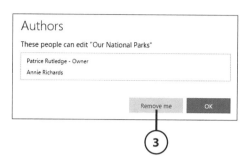

My Sways Page

The All Sways page is renamed back to My Sways if you remove all shared Sways.

Embedding a Sway

As you discovered in Chapter 4, "Embedding Content in a Sway," you can use an embed code to add content to your Sway from an external source such as Vimeo, Vine, or SoundCloud. In addition to embedding content in a Sway, you can also embed a Sway itself in an external site such as a website or blog. Sway even enables you to embed a Sway in another Sway.

Embed a Sway on a Website or Blog

One of the most popular uses of a Sway embed code is to embed a Sway on a website or blog. In this example, you embed a Sway on a WordPress site. The steps are similar if you used another tool or service to create your site. You can embed a Sway anywhere that allows embedding an <iframe> code.

1. Click the Share button.

2. Select the Share option if it isn't already selected.

3. Click the Show More (…) button.

4. Click Get Embed Code.

5. Copy the code in the Embed This Sway box (Ctrl+C).

6. Click Close.

7. In WordPress, open the post or page where you want to embed the Sway.

8. Click the Text tab.

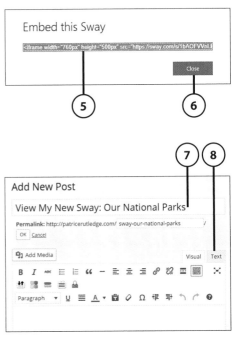

9. Paste (Ctrl+V) the code you copied into the text box.

Next Steps

After adding any additional content, click the Preview button to preview your Sway on the Web or click the Publish button to publish the post or page with the embedded Sway.

View a Sway on the Web

Before publishing an embedded Sway online, you should preview it to understand what your viewers will see and verify that there aren't any problems.

1. Navigate the Sway by either scrolling (vertical layout) or clicking arrows (horizontal or optimized for presentation layouts).

2. Click Made with Sway to open the Sway in a separate browser window.

3. Click the Share This Sway Socially icon to share the Sway on popular social sites.

Social Sharing Options

Social sharing options include sharing to Facebook, Twitter, Yammer, LinkedIn, Pinterest, Google+, and more. You can also copy an embed code to embed this Sway on another site.

4. Click the Fullscreen icon to open the Sway fullscreen.

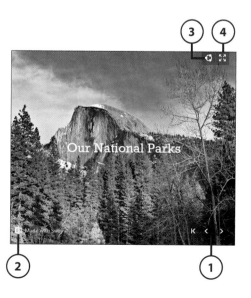

Embed a Sway in Another Sway

A final option is to embed a Sway in another Sway. For example, you might want to showcase a series of related Sways in a single Sway, such as those created by a company, organization, or school.

1. In the Sway you want to embed, click the Share button.

2. Select the Share option if it isn't already selected.

3. Click the Show More (…) button.

4. Click Get Embed Code.

5. Copy the code in the Embed This Sway box (Ctrl+C).

6. Click Close.

7. Click Sway.

8. Click the Sway in which you want to embed the first Sway.

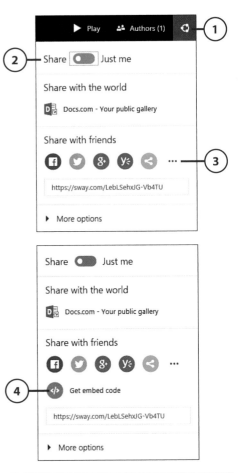

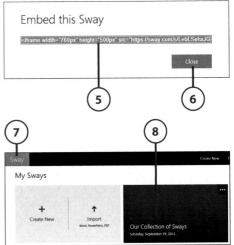

9. Click the Cards tab.

10. Drag the Embed Card to the storyline.

11. Paste (Ctrl+V) your embed code on the card.

12. Click Preview.

13. Click View.

14. The embedded Sway displays on the canvas.

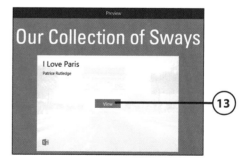

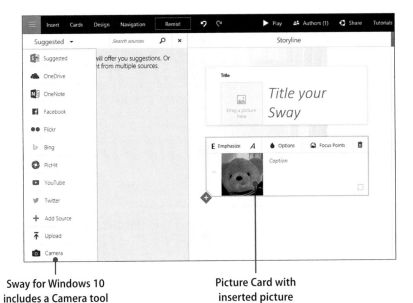

Sway for Windows 10
includes a Camera tool

Picture Card with
inserted picture

In this chapter, you explore the Sway for Windows 10 app. Specific topics in this chapter include the following:

→ Exploring Sway for Windows 10

→ Installing Sway for Windows 10

→ Taking and inserting a picture

9

Installing and Using Sway for Windows 10

Sway for Windows 10 is the Sway app that's designed specifically for Windows 10. Although the primary audience for this app is Windows 10 tablet users, it's also available for download on any Windows 10 PC.

Exploring Sway for Windows 10

The Sway for Windows 10 app is nearly identical to the Sway Web-based app. Here are the main differences:

- **More Options menu**—The More Options menu is on the left side of the screen rather than on the right.

**The More Options
menu is on the left**

**Your existing Sways are
available to view and edit**

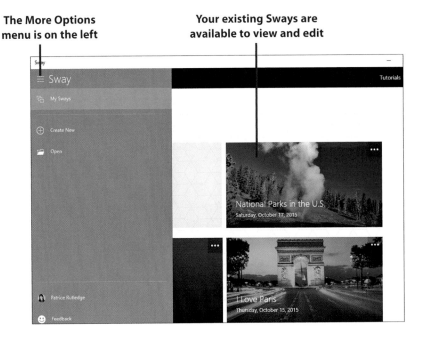

- **New Sway limitations**—Although you can create a new Sway from scratch, you can't create a Sway by importing content. You need to use the Web-based Sway app to do that.

Your only option is to create
a Sway from scratch

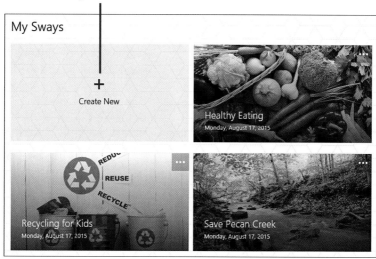

- **Camera tool**—The Camera tool is available from the Suggested drop-down list. This enables you to use the built-in camera on your Windows device to take a picture and insert it on a Picture Card on your Sway storyline. See "Taking and Inserting a Picture" later in this chapter.

- **Offline access**—You can access your Sways offline if you don't have Internet or Wi-Fi access. This enables you to present a Sway to an audience without worrying about connectivity.

- **Multiple account access**—Stay logged into multiple Sway accounts on the same device.

It's Not All Good

Watch for Cloud Content in an Offline Sway

Be aware that if your Sway includes Google Maps, YouTube videos, or other cloud-hosted content, this content won't display without access to the Internet. Be sure to test your Sway offline before presenting it online to an audience.

Installing Sway for Windows 10

You can download and install Sway for Windows 10 from the Windows Store.

Install Sway for Windows 10

Installing Sway for Windows 10 takes just a few minutes.

1. Navigate to the Windows Store at this site: https://www.microsoft.com/en-us/store/apps/sway/9wzdncrd2g0j.

2. Click the Install button.

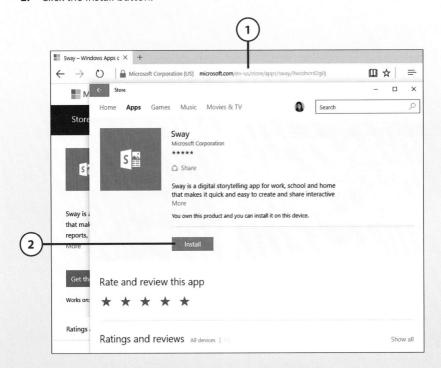

App Requirements

If you want to install the Sway for Windows 10 app on your computer, you must upgrade to Windows 10 first. If you're using a computer with an earlier operating system, the Upgrade to Windows 10 link will prompt you to upgrade first.

3. Wait while the Sway app downloads and installs.

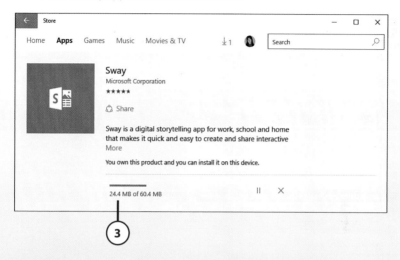

4. Notice that a notification informs you when installation is complete.

5. Click the Open button.

6. Sway for Windows 10 displays.

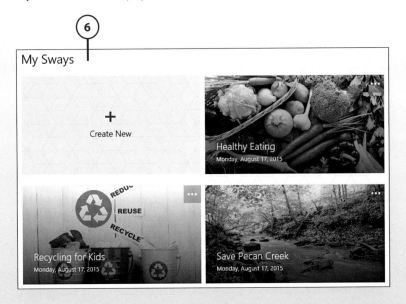

Existing Sways

If you've already created any Sways using the Web-based Sway app, they also display on the My Sways page of Sway for Windows 10.

Installation Alternative

Another way to install this app is to navigate to https://sway.com, and then scroll down and click the Windows 10 button.

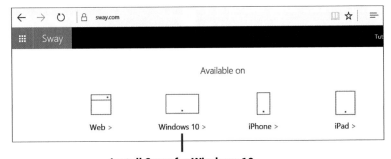

**Install Sway for Windows 10
from the Sway website**

Taking and Inserting a Picture

The ability to take and insert a picture using your device's built-in camera is one of the best features of the Sway for Windows 10 app. You can take a picture of yourself from a desktop device or use your tablet as a camera.

Take and Insert a Picture

You can take and add a picture to your Sway in just a few minutes.

1. Create or open a Sway, and then tap the Insert tab.

2. Select Camera from the drop-down list.

3. Tap the Camera icon to take a picture.

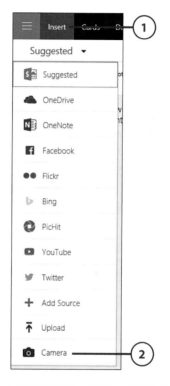

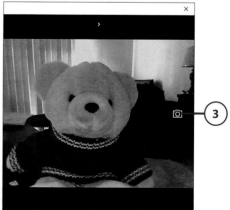

4. Drag your picture to fit in the cropping window.

Zoom In and Out

Use the zoom button in the lower-right corner to adjust what displays in your picture.

5. Optionally, tap See More to display descriptions below each button.

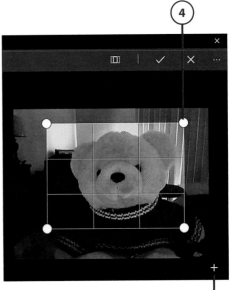

Zoom in
and out

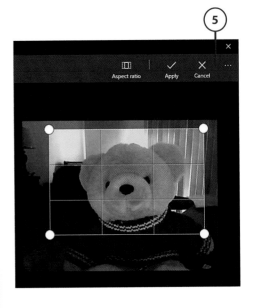

6. Tap Aspect Ratio to select a different aspect ratio.

What Is Aspect Ratio?

Aspect ratio is the proportion between the width and height of a picture. For example, 4 inches by 3 inches is an aspect ratio for a rectangular picture. Options include Widescreen, Square, and several specific sizes. Select Original to return to your original ratio.

7. Tap Apply to save your picture.

Start Over

If you don't like your picture and want to start over, tap Cancel.

8. Sway displays the picture on the Picture Card.

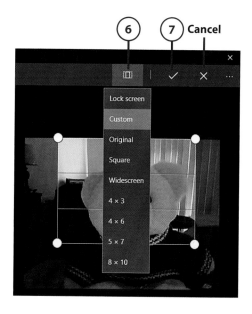

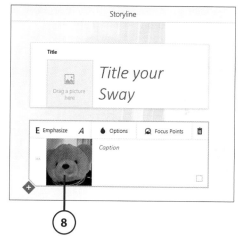

Quickly try out a new Sway
style using the iPad app

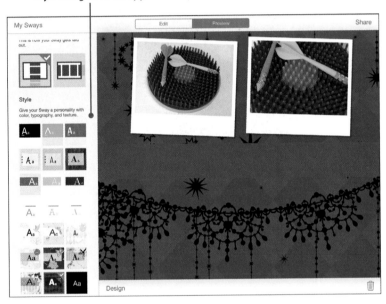

In this chapter, you explore Sway for the iPhone and iPad. Specific topics in this chapter include the following:

→ Getting to know Sway for iPhone and iPad

→ Installing Sway for iPhone and iPad

10

Installing and Using Sway for iPhone and iPad

Sway for iPhone and iPad is the Sway app that's designed specifically for iOS mobile device users.

Getting to Know Sway for iPhone and iPad

In this section, you explore the differences between Sway on the Web and Sway on your iPhone or iPad, including how to navigate the Sway app on iOS devices.

Explore Sway for iPhone and iPad

Sway for iPhone and iPad is very similar to the Sway Web-based app, but there are a few differences. These include the following:

- **More Options menu**—The More Options menu is on the left side of the screen rather than on the right.

- **New Sway limitations**—Although you can create a new Sway, you can't create a Sway by importing content. You need to use the Web-based Sway app to do that.

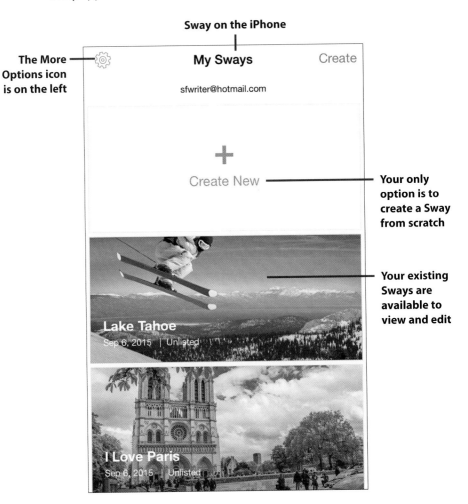

Sway on the iPhone

The More Options icon is on the left

My Sways

sfwriter@hotmail.com

Create

Create New — Your only option is to create a Sway from scratch

Your existing Sways are available to view and edit

Lake Tahoe
Sep 6, 2015 | Unlisted

I Love Paris
Sep 6, 2015 | Unlisted

Sway on the iPad

The More Options icon is on the left

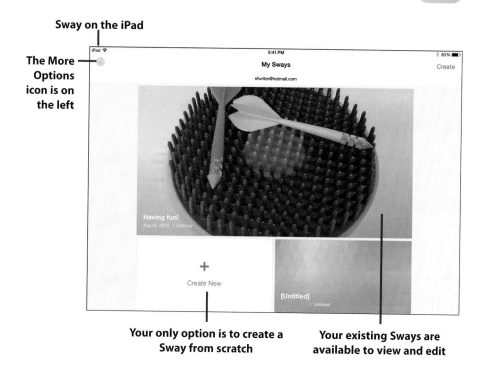

Your only option is to create a Sway from scratch

Your existing Sways are available to view and edit

- **Camera tool**—You can use the built-in camera on your iPhone or iPad to take a picture and insert it on your Sway storyline.

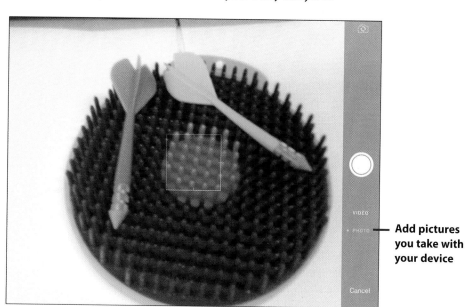

Add pictures you take with your device

Navigate Sway for iPhone and iPad

If you've been using Sway on the Web, Sway for iPhone and iPad offers similar functionality but in a different interface.

When you create or edit a Sway, the Edit screen opens. This screen includes five buttons for adding content to your Sway:

- **Media**—Add a picture stored on your device.

- **Camera**—Insert a picture you take with your device's built-in camera.

- **Text**—Add and format text.

- **Header**—Add header text and an optional picture.

- **More**—View additional card options such as Group and Stack.

Edit screen on the iPad

**Add content with
these buttons**

When you're ready to preview your work or move on to additional formatting options, tap Preview at the top of the screen. From this screen, you can view your Sway as well as access additional options such as Remix!, navigation, and styles, which you learned about earlier in this book.

Edit button

Editing a Sway on an iPhone

Preview button

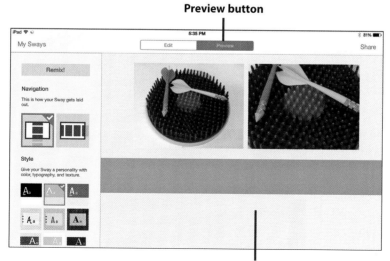

Previewing a Sway on an iPad

Preview button

Previewing a Sway on an iPhone

Installing Sway for iPhone and iPad

You can download and install Sway for iPhone and iPad from the App Store.

Install Sway for iPhone and iPad

Installing Sway for iPhone and iPad takes just a few minutes. In this example, you install the Sway app on an iPad. Installing Sway on an iPhone is similar.

1. Tap the App Store icon on your Home screen.

2. Tap Search and type **Office Sway** in the Search box.

3. Tap the Get button to open the Sway app.

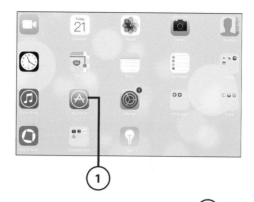

4. Tap the Sign in to Start button.

5. Type the email address associated with your Microsoft account. Optionally, you can enter the phone number associated with this account.

6. Tap Next.

7. Type your password.

8. Tap Sign In.

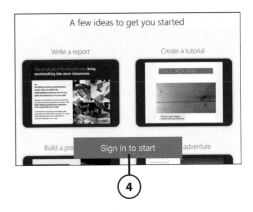

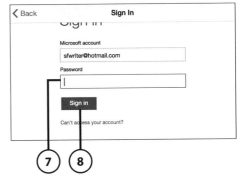

9. The My Sways page opens.

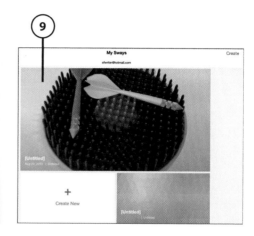

Installation Alternatives

Another way to install this app is to navigate to https://sway.com, scroll down the page, and click either the iPhone button or the iPad button. Optionally, you can navigate directly to https://itunes.apple.com/app/id929856545.

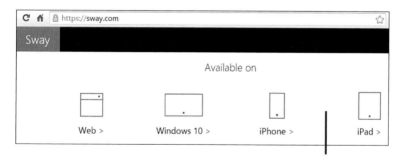

Install Sway for the iPhone and iPad from the Sway website

Index

D

S

More Best-Selling **My** Books!

Learning to use your smartphone, tablet, camera, game, or software has never been easier with the full-color My Series. You'll find simple, step-by-step instructions from our team of experienced authors. The organized, task-based format allows you to quickly and easily find exactly what you want to achieve.

Visit quepublishing.com/mybooks to learn more.

REGISTER THIS PRODUCT
SAVE 35%*
ON YOUR NEXT PURCHASE!

⌨ How to Register Your Product

- Go to quepublishing.com/register
- Sign in or create an account
- Enter ISBN: 10- or 13-digit ISBN that appears on the back cover of your product

🔓 Benefits of Registering

- Ability to download product updates
- Access to bonus chapters and workshop files
- A 35% coupon to be used on your next purchase – valid for 30 days
  To obtain your coupon, click on "Manage Codes" in the right column of your Account page
- Receive special offers on new editions and related Que products

Please note that the benefits for registering may vary by product. Benefits will be listed on your Account page under Registered Products.

We value and respect your privacy. Your email address will not be sold to any third party company.

* 35% discount code presented after product registration is valid on most print books, eBooks, and full-course videos sold on QuePublishing.com. Discount may not be combined with any other offer and is not redeemable for cash. Discount code expires after 30 days from the time of product registration. Offer subject to change.

quepublishing.com

My Office Sway

Copyright © 2016 by Pearson Education, Inc.

ISBN-13: 978-0-7897-5543-8
ISBN-10: 0-7897-5543-2

Library of Congress Control Number: 2015950786

Printed in the United States of America

First Printing: November 2015

Trademarks

All terms mentioned in this book that are known to be trademarks or service marks have been appropriately capitalized. Que Publishing cannot attest to the accuracy of this information. Use of a term in this book should not be regarded as affecting the validity of any trademark or service mark.

Warning and Disclaimer

Every effort has been made to make this book as complete and as accurate as possible, but no warranty or fitness is implied. The information provided is on an "as is" basis. The author and the publisher shall have neither liability nor responsibility to any person or entity with respect to any loss or damages arising from the information contained in this book.

Special Sales

For information about buying this title in bulk quantities, or for special sales opportunities (which may include electronic versions; custom cover designs; and content particular to your business, training goals, marketing focus, or branding interests), please contact our corporate sales department at corpsales@pearsoned.com or (800) 382-3419.

For government sales inquiries, please contact governmentsales@pearsoned.com.

For questions about sales outside the U.S., please contact international@pearsoned.com.

Editor-in-Chief
Greg Wiegand

Acquisitions Editor
Michelle Newcomb

Development Editor
Joyce Nielsen

Managing Editor
Sandra Schroeder

Senior Project Editor
Tonya Simpson

Copy Editor
Anne Goebel

Indexer
Lisa Stumpf

Proofreader
Debbie Williams

Technical Editor
Christopher Parent

Publishing Coordinator
Cindy Teeters

Cover Designer
Mark Shirar

Compositor
Bumpy Design

My
Office Sway

Patrice-Anne Rutledge

QUE

800 East 96th Street
Indianapolis, Indiana 46240 USA